Judy Benowitz's "Boater-Head" places the reader in an "I've been there" moment. It is funny, wise, and timely, and it fits well within her latest anthology of short stories. Benowitz's *Descendants* takes you through time and from one end of the world to another. No spoilers from me, though. Read it for yourself and enjoy the journey.

Carol Roddenberry, artist and writer

Award-winning writer Judy Benowitz has her roots in the deep South, where she was influenced and often frustrated by her strong-willed mother—a woman ahead of her time who served in the armed forces during World War II, married a hometown boy, and, along the way, had a long-time, long-distance admirer.

Added to the colorful mix is a large family that Benowitz brings to life with all their virtues and flaws. In "Pal O My Heart," her portrayals of these characters from an often-misunderstood culture ring true to this reader, also a child of the 1950s and 1960s South.

Before bringing her readers up to date on her adventures as a modern Baptist-turned-Jewish wife and mother who uses high tech to maintain family ties and lovingly supports to her son on the painful road to showbiz success, she leads the audience through her days as an activist during political upheaval of the 1960s and worldwide travel as an airline stewardess dubbed "Legs Benowitz" by her admiring co-workers.

Benowitz's recollections of her life so far are touching, funny, surprising, heartbreaking, suspenseful, and more. Pour your favorite cocktail and prepare to be entertained. It's a great yarn!

Donna B. Jones, writer and editor, Austin

In December 2021, Judy Benowitz sat down to share her family's story with the Museum of History and Holocaust Education (MHHE) at Kennesaw State University. In the spring of 2022, the MHHE will display photographs and artifacts from the Benowitz/Harris/Coker collection in their *Georgia Journeys and Beyond Rosie: Women in World War II* exhibits.

Coupled with stories shared in Benowitz's oral history and memoirs, these artifacts paint a picture of a family with deep roots in Georgia whose members served across the United States and around the world during World War II. This service broadened their perspective and helped to shape how the next generations would approach education, career, and the telling of their American story.

Adina Jocelyn Langer
Curator, Museum of History and Holocaust Education

DESCENDANTS

Judy Benowitz

TREATY OAK PUBLISHERS

Publisher's Note

Copyright © 2022 by Judy Benowitz
All rights reserved.

No part of this book may be reproduced, scanned, or distributed in any printed or electronic form without permission from the author. Please do not participate in or encourage piracy of copyrighted materials in violation of the author's rights. Purchase only authorized editions.

Printed and published in the United States of America

Treaty Oak Publishers

ISBN-978-1-943658-94-7

Available in print from Amazon

Grateful acknowledgment is made to the publications in which these stories first appear: "Nursing Home Cafeteria" in *Grits* (*Girls Raised in the South*); "Pal O' My Heart" in *The Walton Tribune* and *National Women's History Museum* and *Brush Brooms and Straw Ticks*; "My Son the Actor" in *Atlanta Jewish Times*; "Boater-Head" won first place in the *Georgia Writers Museum's* 2015 Creative Writing Contest; "The Descendants" in *Heroically Well Adjusted*; "Zoom Passover" in The Bartow History Museum, Cartersville, Georgia; "Marilyn" in *Hindsight* anthology.

FOR MY FAMILY

Table of Contents

Introduction - 1

Pal O' My Heart - 3

The 1960s - 31

Old Cars - 39

Atlanta and the Age of Aquarius - 43

The Vietnam War Protest - 47

The Finest-Looking Man I Ever Met - 57

Legs Benowitz - 63

My Son the Actor - 97

Boater-Head - 105

The Jewish Mom - 109

Israel - 113

From Istanbul with Love - 117

Nursing Home Cafeteria - 141

Descendants - 143

Zoom Passover - 157

Marilyn - 161

Acknowledgments - 169

Introduction

To write the story of your life—to write any story, really, to put words to the page in an attempt to say something true—takes an enormous act of courage. And courageous is a word that easily describes my mother, Judy Benowitz. For the past eight years, I have witnessed her labor over her memoir, writing, revising, rewriting, restructuring, workshopping, considering the vantage point from which the story should be told, where it should begin and where it should end, finishing a draft only to start all over again.

The writer's endless toil, a pursuit the two of us share. Along the way, she's published stories in anthologies, literary journals, magazines and newspapers. She also went back to school at the age of sixty-five to pursue her Master of Arts in Professional Writing from Kennesaw State University—an act of bravery, in and of itself, and a lesson I cherish in our infinite capacity for reinvention.

I remember the evening when she first gave a dramatic reading—because these things must be done with drama in the Benowitz household—of her essay "Pal O' My Heart," which opens this collection. My younger sister, brother and I were back in Cartersville, the small town in Georgia where my parents have made a home for over twenty-five years, probably for a Thanksgiving holiday, having flown in from the homes we were now making in Miami, New York, and L.A. We sat on the dock overlooking the Etowah River in the backyard at dusk as my mom told the story of a twenty-six-year-old Navy WAVE in Washington D.C. from rural Georgia and the mystery Navy man she corresponded with by letter throughout World War II. It was the story of her mother, my grandmother, Ivah Ree Coker, which she had exhumed from our basement in a bundle of letters, documents and photographs, along with Ivah Ree's Navy-issued gabardine raincoat and hat.

In the opening scene, my mother cradles these personal effects of her deceased mother in her arms like a baby. As she read her essay to us on the dock that evening, with the misty sky above the river changing from fiery orange-red to dun, we found ourselves teary-eyed at the evocation of this plucky young woman, our grandmother, whom we had only known as elderly and frail, imagining what life had been like for her and recognizing character traits that felt familiar to who we were today. Later in the collection, in "Nursing Home Cafeteria," we meet Ivah Ree again, only now she is wheelchair-bound at the end of her life, cradled in my mother's arms once more.

This collection is called *Descendants* for the essay of the same name that chronicles the history and family tree of the William Harris Homestead, a plantation in Monroe, Georgia that dates back circa 1825 and has been preserved on the National Register of Historic Places, from which Ivah Ree and my mother descend. But lineage oozes through every essay. Just as Ivah Ree Harris ran off to Washington D.C. in her twenties to become a woman in uniform, so did Judy Coker thirty years later as a flight attendant for United Airlines. Her uniform was a black, fitted sweater and floor-length plaid skirt buttoned up the front that she wore unbuttoned above the knee, earning her the nickname "Legs Benowitz," which is also the title of the essay that chronicles that wild, independent, jet set period of her life before starting a family.

Another thirty years later and Kristy Benowitz, her middle child, would don a red hijab as a flight attendant for Emirates Airlines in Dubai, which she recalls in "From Istanbul With Love," a travelogue that also explores the Jewish diaspora from which my father, Robert Benowitz, is descended. My mother pursued acting in Southern California and did community theater productions with my brother Brett and me as kids in Cartersville.

Today, Brett is following in her footsteps as an actor and musician in LA, a lineage she examines in "My Son the Actor." And one year after she graduated from her masters program at Kennesaw, I found the inspiration to move back to New York to pursue the MFA in Writing that I had always wanted at Sarah Lawrence College after a near decade working as a freelance travel writer and journalist in Miami. This is the impact of a mother. This is the way inheritance works. And it's the impulse of the memoirist to seek out these patterns, to piece them together, to try to make art out of the seeming chaos, randomness and sweetness of life.

That's what my mother has done in this collection. We witness a woman's coming of age in the South, from the tumultuous Civil Rights era and the integration of her high school in the 1960s to Vietnam War protests and the hippie counterculture in her college days in 1970s Atlanta. It's there that she meets my father and falls in love, propelling her life in a completely new direction.

She would now straddle two different cultures, her past and future in constant tension, from the dark, entrenched history of the South to the dazzling new frontier of Southern California, from a Southern Baptist childhood to a conversion to Judaism, from a wild child career girl to motherhood and domesticity. Through her eyes, we also witness our country's coming of age over the second half of the twentieth century with all its fits and starts and violence, which shines a light on where we are today.

And after twenty years in California where Kristy, Brett and I were all born and raised, her story and her life would return her to Georgia, her rootedness in the South's red clay soil inescapable. The dualities of my mother's life are also a part of my siblings' and my inheritance.

Sure, my mother has been working on her memoirs for years, but she's been a storyteller my entire life and surely before then. From writing songs about me and Kristy and Brett and the family dog when we were kids ("Who is this baby girl / that I love so much? / Her name is Shayne / I'll never complain / She's my baby girl, my sweet baby girl") to short stories that chronicled our childhood, there are pages and pages of old typewritten manuscripts in the basement inside a desk that my father built in the 1970s painted with red and black peace signs.

That's the same basement where she unearthed her mother's letters and documents that would become "Pal O' My Heart." And I have my own dusty manuscripts in that basement, from college and my early years in New York, before I would set off on my own adventure in pursuit of travel and the writer's life.

"Mother had a way of taking the fear out of life," my mother writes of Ivah Ree in *Descendants*. It's a characteristic that she also inherited. A lineage continues and it's worth examining and recording. Since she began working in earnest on this collection in the summer of 2020, she would tell me, "Someone has to record these stories or the memories of these people and their way of life will disappear forever."

Every family should be so lucky to have a storyteller, a chronicler, someone to record their history and preserve it for posterity. The story of my mother's life—where she came from, where she's been and the people and places she has loved and lost along the way—is preserved here.

Shayne Benowitz
journalist, travel writer, essayist

ULYSSES

by Alfred Tennyson

I cannot rest from travel: I will drink
Life to the lees: all times I have enjoy'd
Greatly, have suffer'd greatly, both with those
That loved me, and alone…

I am a part of all that I have met…
As tho' to breath were life! Life piled on life
Were all too little, and of one to me
Little remains….

Pal O' My Heart

(1943-1945)
A biography

I carried Mother's World War II Navy-issued raincoat from the basement along with a publication by the WWII Navy WAVES, of which she was a member.

"Mother," I said, as I opened the door to the living room, speaking to her as if she were standing at the top of the stairs.

"Did you hear what I just said?" I said to my husband, who sat in his recliner, watching TV.

He glanced at me.

"I called you Mother. I meant to say Bob, but I said Mother."

"Well, you're carrying her in your arms," he said.

I inhaled the scent of the coat I held like a baby as it draped across my shoulder—the rich smell of aged gabardine, but no smell of her remained.

"I have her hat, too, you know."

Taking my bundle, including pictures from WWII, into my bedroom, I found Mother's uniform hat with its "Property of the Navy Reserves" tag and another tag with her name on it: I.R. Harris—Ivah Ree.

Tears pricked my eyes as I remembered the frail woman who was once so strong. A deeply religious woman given to cursing—'shitass' being one of her favorite expressions to describe someone. She could out-preach any man of the cloth who came through the Mountain Creek Baptist Church in Monroe, Georgia, where she belonged and sang in the choir in her off-key alto voice, ever searching for the harmony.

She wrote the Mountain Creek Baptist Church News for the local paper—a journalist in her own right who raised two writers: my sister Valerie, who was a freelance writer, and me, a creative writer now documenting Ivah Ree's biography—Ivah Ree Harris, US Navy WAVE.

Navy Women— The WAVES

The United States Naval Reserve (Women's Reserve), better known under the acronym WAVES for Women Accepted for Volunteer Emergency Service, was established in July 1942. It authorized the US Navy to accept women into the Naval Reserves as commissioned officers and at the enlisted level for the duration of the war plus six months.

Although the notion of women in the Navy was not widely supported by Congress or the Navy, through the efforts of First Lady Eleanor Roosevelt, among others, The Women's Armed Services Integration Act laid the groundwork.

Lieutenant Commander Mildred H. McAfee became the first director of the WAVES. McAfee was on leave from her position as president of Wellesley College and was an experienced and highly respected educator.

As she set about recruiting WAVES, McAfee primarily used radio and newspaper advertising, posters, brochures, and personal contacts. Advertising that met her standards for good taste focused on patriotism and the need for women to take positions that would free up male servicemen for combat duty. By 1945 the WAVES' ranks included 8,475 officers and 73,816 enlisted.

At first, WAVES officers served in administrative and support roles, although many later served as attorneys and engineers. Numerous enlisted women became aviation mechanics.

As time went by, WAVES served in 1,000 shore stations in the United States, releasing 70,000 men for combat by taking over their routine jobs. In assignments such as Navy storekeeping, clerical work, and stenography, the Navy women were at least as competent as Navy men. They briefed Navy pilots on the weather, posted weather observations and forecasts, and directed air traffic from flying fields control towers. They served as metalsmiths, radio operators, aviation machinist's mates, truck drivers, laboratory technicians, decoders, and cooks. In the 1,000 Naval installations in the United States, half of them were WAVES at work.

Because of WAVES Director McAfee's academic background, training camps were set up on college campuses. In February 1943, the largest permanent boot camp for all enlistees was Hunter College in the Bronx in New York City. With a six-week training, new classes of 1,600 women arrived every two weeks. That same year, Ivah Ree took her training at Hunter College. More than a half century later, when I interviewed Ivah Ree on 8 mm film in 2000, she told me she had wanted to be a flight attendant, but at that time flight attendants were nurses, so she joined the armed services instead.

In March 1945, *Time Magazine* described the training Ivah Ree and the other WAVES underwent at Hunter College:

> In those six weeks they became trim and sharp—factory-made old salts who referred to walls as bulkheads, windows as ports, and floors as decks. They absorbed Navy tradition, had a quick but thorough briefing on naval operation, naval weapons, history, and current affairs.
> They were also imbued with the idea that if a WAVE quit, it was the same as a battlefront casualty.
>
> Miss Mac - TIME
Time Magazine
Monday March 12, 1945, Vol. XLV No. 11,

While going through a box in my basement, my share of memorabilia that my sister Valerie and I divided when Mother died in 2002, I found "Pass in Review Review!"—a 20-page illustrated brochure describing the community in which Ivah Ree lived after her training at Hunter College—WAVE Quarters D, the largest WAVE quarters in America, located at Massachusetts and Nebraska Avenues in Washington, DC. It is the single best archive I have of Ivah Ree's career in the WAVES, including her handwritten notes on the publication's photographs. The back page lists her name:

Logging in with Ivah Ree Harris
Billet Barracks 14-137
1943-? She logged in.

In the opening page of the brochure is a description of the life as a member of the WAVES in Washington, DC. Ivah Ree underlined and commented on things that interested her.

She was a country girl from a large family of seven children who grew up in rural Monroe, Georgia. Her parents were farmers, so she could relate to "the fresh country tang" and "the rain-cleansed air"—phrases that she underlined in the script. She also underlined "change of watches at the front gate," as if she enjoyed the responsibility.

She put quotes around, "Specialists," which was her rating and "This is our world today!" because it described her life there for two years. At the bottom of the page, Ivah Ree wrote "Ain't that touching." She could be sarcastic when things got mushy, although she had warm memories of her friends Coonce and Jennings—the last names of two women who served with her and with whom she corresponded all her life. I remember their letters on the top of the TV in the living room where I grew up.

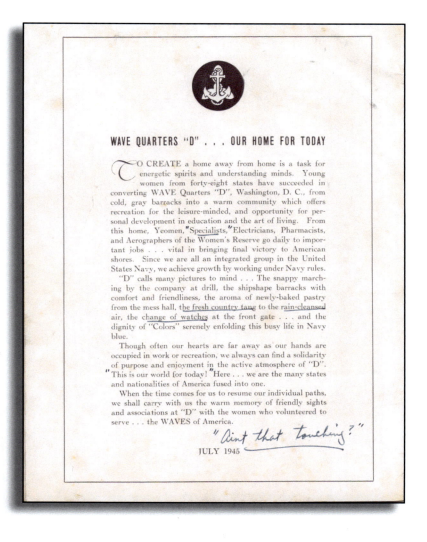

Ivah Ree's rating was Specialist: Sp(Q)3c., a specialist third class. The WAVES were under oath to maintain strict secrecy even after cessation of hostilities, and there were serious heavy penalties for violation, as described in the III. Duties Performed section in her Rating Description.

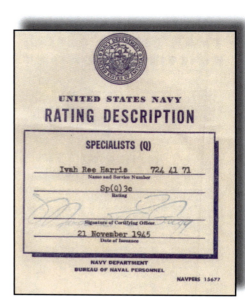

In my interview with her in 2000 at age 86, she talked about her job in communications. She took messages, not knowing what all the communications meant, and she was not allowed to discuss them, in the same way as the women in Denise Kiernan's biography, The Girls of Atomic City: The Untold Story of the Women Who Helped Win WWII.

The girls of Atomic City were sworn to secrecy and risked severe penalties for violating the oath by talking about their job, which was to build the atomic bomb. They did not know what they were building until the bomb dropped.

Ivah Ree, however, was one of the first to know when the war ended because she copied the first White House press release when President Truman declared victory over Japan on V-J Day, August 15, 1945.

"There was a bomb," she said. "The streets were mobbed, and the transportation shut down in Washington, DC, because the war ended that day. My roommates and I caught a ride in a private car."

" 'Try not to get separated,' I told Coonce and Jennings, 'or we'll never make it back to the barracks,' which was far away. Everyone was kissing everyone. One sailor came up to me and wanted to thank me for taking his job as a yeoman so he could go to sea. He loved my Southern accent and wanted me to talk to him. We kissed a few times. He said, 'What do you want to do?' I told him, 'I like to dance.' So we danced in the street while the crowds rushed past us."

I asked Mother, in my interview, if she could have been in the famous kiss in Times Square documented in a photograph published in *Life Magazine*.

"Yes," she said, "any of us could have been."

Without showing every picture in the "Pass and Review" brochure, I can tell you that Ivah Ree liked to swim in the Olympic-sized pool. In the picture of "The Ship's Fountain," a favorite "hangout any time of day," the counters are filled with WAVES eating ice cream floats. Ivah Ree writes, "Always Crowded."

She enjoyed the Sailorette Theatre, where Naturally Navy, a musical performed with sparkle and saltiness, featured numbers that reflected their world: "Hi Honolulu," "Naturally Navy," "Salty Sue," "Embarkation Blues," and "Dream Crazy." A capacity house, including distinguished blue and gold braid, acclaimed Naturally Navy a natural.

Also pictured in the brochure is a bus loading for "Dances at Fort Meade (free transportation), Navy Meets Army!"

"Some fun this," Ivah Ree wrote under the picture.

Mother loved to dance. She enjoyed a reputation for cutting the rug. I can still see her dancing in the living room, her dark hair permed into soft curls, her black, pointy-rimmed cat-eye glasses alight her little, pointed nose, her head down, and arms up as her hips swayed to the music. Her bare feet stamped intricate choreography onto the wood floor. I didn't know the dance—the fox trot or turkey in the straw—but the music was in her. She wore a house dress that was a shift, but it clung to her hour-glass figure—a little overweight by then, but still shapely.

She was a 'sweater girl'. That is how she described herself. It was a saying from the World War II era of men. Buxom women were referred to as 'sweater girls'. That was the fashion back then: a thin sweater worn with a straight skirt.

In this picture, Ivah Ree wears the hat I inherited. She was 26. The uniform was made especially for WAVES, designed by the noted New York fashion house of Mainbocher. Mrs. James V. Forrestal, wife of the assistant secretary of the Navy, secured their design services. The winter uniform was made from navy blue wool, worn with a white shirt and dark blue tie. The jacket was single breasted and unbelted with a six-gored skirt. Included were black oxfords and plain black pumps, a brimmed hat, black gloves, black leather purse, and rain and winter coats. The summer uniform was similar but in lighter fabric. Later, a gray-and-white striped seersucker work uniform for summer was added, along with slacks and dungarees.

The following pictures from "Pass in Review!" show notes written by Ivah Ree that give more insight to her personality. She points out her barracks in one photo, and other pictures include her bunk room and the mess hall. The brochure tells the story of life in WAVE Quarters D.

AIR VIEW OF WAVE QUARTERS "D" reveals its well-planned pattern, so harmonious with the ordered design of Washington. Complete with streets connecting barracks to barracks, cross-walks, and the key administration, recreation, and commissary buildings, "D" is indeed a community. At the upper left is familiar Ward Circle

CUBICLE... planned for living!... enjoying!... relaxing!

QUARTERDECK takes the barracks' business in its stride.

LAUNDRY ROOM facilities keep white shirts in circulation.   LOCKER... convenient and compact... displays stowage of gear.

BARRACKS LOUNGE... finest atmosphere to write to Mom and GI Joe... enjoy potato chips and cokes... "shoot the breeze."

DESCENDANTS ❖ 13

TIME FOR MESS . . . proclaimed by the clock . . . starts one of the four daily treks of Navy personnel to the GI mess hall.

WAVE-SIZED MEAL assembled from salad to dessert through the efficient teamwork of the many girls "on the line."

BAKERY, with WAVES manning big-scale equipment, turns out such delicacies as Parkerhouse rolls and Boston cream pie.

The ole line again!

navy plates

Two WAVES attack the appetizing, well-balanced meal on their traditional "tin" trays with an "all out" enthusiasm.

VAST MESS HALL . . . shipshape after swabbing . . . when the work of serving thousands is done for another day!

The ole well known mess hall!

Pal O' My Heart
(1936-1943)

When Ivah Ree Harris graduated Monroe High School in 1936, she went to work at the Winder Barrow Manufacturing Plant in Winder, Georgia. She bought a brand new, black Chevy that she drove to Atlanta to shop at Rich's Department Store, a Southern institution, with her girlfriends Dovie and Margie.

"Let's go to Woolworths and get a Coke," Dovie said, after a long day of walking the city streets.

A group of sailors in white uniforms passed the girls and looked back at them. One of them winked at Ivah Ree.

"Follow those guys," Ivah Ree said. "I love a man in uniform,"

The three girls followed the men into Woolworths and sat at the counter. The men wasted no time in joining them.

"What are you girls up to today? You look thirsty," the handsome man with the mustache said to Ivah Ree. "Let me buy you a Coke,"

"I'd like a chocolate milk shake," Ivah Ree said, as she stared into his blue eyes.

"One chocolate milk shake coming up."

He ordered the milk shake, and the other sailors ordered Cokes for Dovie and Margie. "My name is Goldman Frase. Who are you?"

"Ivah Ree Harris."

"Ivah Ree. Pretty name."

"You have the prettiest blue eyes," she said.

"Thank you." He leaned in closer to her.

"Where are you stationed?" she said.

"I'm based in Seattle, Washington."

"Where are you from?" Ivah Ree batted her eyelashes.

"Tennessee. I'm home on leave. You?"

"Monroe, about an hour drive. We came shopping."

They talked and laughed the afternoon away, until Goldman had to catch his bus to Tennessee.

"Can I write to you? I ship out in two days. I don't know for how long."

He held her hand and kissed it.

Ivah Ree wrote her address on a napkin and put it into Goldman's chest pocket.

"Write to me, sailor." She patted his chest.

They walked outside, and Goldman embraced Ivah Ree, kissing her good-bye. She watched him go down the sidewalk with his buddies dressed in their uniform whites, a lovely sight.

This chance encounter with Goldman could have taken place in Savannah, or at a dance in Athens, Georgia. I found pictures of Mother shopping in Atlanta, and in another photo she stood by the Savannah sign—places she could have met a sailor on leave. Goldman was from McMinn, Tennessee, near Knoxville, so he might have gone dancing in Athens. Since I don't know how they met, I imagined the possibilities.

The fact is that Goldman Frase wrote to Ivah Ree for five years, sending her Christmas cards and pictures of his time at sea.

Her first letter from Goldman was a Christmas card in 1937 from Seattle, Washington.

Every day she waited by the mailbox for its delivery, with a 1½ cent stamp of President Warren G. Harding on the envelope and a reminder to mail early for Christmas. "Best Wishes for Christmas," the card reads, with no personal inscription inside.

The next year, in 1938, with a 3-cent stamp and Thomas Jefferson 1801-1809 pictured, Goldman wrote from Long Beach, California.

Inside the Christmas card he penned: "I've hunted and hunted. I cannot find the card I want to bestow all the blessings I wish to bestow upon you this coming year."

In April of 1938, he sent a snapshot from Honolulu, with an inscription on the back:

"Just trying to keep beer cold." (Goldman is on the right)

On April 25, 1940, he wrote to her from the USS WASP, Boston, Massachusetts. Included was a brochure on the ship and photos of Goldman.

On December 21, 1940, from Portsmouth, Virginia, he wrote again.

"To the one I love at Christmas," the card reads.

He was a football player and served on the *USS Maryland*.

On the back of this picture, dressed in Navy white, he wrote:

"This sweater was given to me for playing football. See five bars-each year playing. Will send large picture with the whole group wearing them. Guantanamo Bay, Cuba. Feb. 1939."

On the back of this photograph, Goldman wrote: "Here's the picture of those *Maryland* football players. How cute they are. Look especially at the one with the mustache. The two in the middle with hats on—one is in charge of the ship—one with 4 bars on his shoulder or Captain, either one with 3 bars are Executive Officers. Both of them swell people—they are not with

us anymore."

The *Maryland* was on Battleship Row at Pearl Harbor during the Japanese attack on December 7, 1941.

At 09:00 when the Japanese attack began, many of the *Maryland*'s crew were eating breakfast or preparing for shore leave. As the first Japanese aircraft appeared and exploded the outboard battleships, the *Maryland*'s bugler blew general quarters. Seaman Leslie Short, who was addressing Christmas cards near his machine gun, was the first to bring his guns into play, shooting down one of two torpedo bombers that had just released on the *USS Oklahoma*, which began to sink.

Because the *Maryland* docked inboard of the *Oklahoma*, she was spared from the initial torpedo attack and managed to bring all her antiaircraft (AA) artillery into action. Survivors from the *Oklahoma* climbed aboard the Maryland. The ship continued to fire after being struck by two armor-piercing bombs that detonated low on her hull. The first made a hole 12 feet by 20 feet in the forecastle awning, and the second exploded the hull at the 22 feet water level, causing flooding.

The ship listed forward by 5 feet. After the attack, firefighting parties from the *Maryland* assisted her compatriots, attempting to rescue survivors from the capsized *Oklahoma*. The men continued to man their AA defenses, in case the Japanese returned to attack. In all, two officers and two men from the *Maryland* were killed in the attack. These were the two officers Goldman pointed out in the picture.

The Japanese reported that the *Maryland* had been sunk, but on December 30, 1941, the battleship entered Puget Sound Navy Yard for repairs along with the *USS Tennessee*. In two months, she was overhauled and by June 1942 was the first ship that had been damaged at Pearl Harbor to return to duty.

On the back of the next photograph, Goldman wrote:

"This only shows one part of the sailors who are all over our ship this way. This picture was taken while we were coming to Islands."

The islands could have been Honolulu, when the *Maryland* entered

Pearl Harbor. The scantily clad men are sunbathing.

On December 21, 1941, just 14 days after Pearl Harbor, Goldman sent a Christmas card to Ivah Ree with a Naval Censor stamp on the envelope. His address was the *USS Salamonie*, New York City, New York.

"Don't know a single wish to send that beats A Merry Christmas, Friend," the card reads with no inscription.

Goldman was not on the *Maryland* at Pearl Harbor, when it was attacked. He knew the men who died according to the report from the *Maryland* battle at sea taken from the Dictionary of American Naval Fighting ships. In his Muster Rolls found on Ancestry.com, he was on the *Maryland* from October 31, 1939, through March 31, 1940. That is when he played football with those men and knew them well. After he left the *Maryland*, his Muster Rolls show he was on the *USS Wasp* from April 25, 1940, until December 31, 1940, before going aboard the USS Salomonie from April 28, 1941, till December 28, 1941.

He wrote to Ivah Ree from the *Wasp,* sending her a pamphlet of the history of the ship and a picture of himself in his white uniform riding a horse. In another photo, he is shown feeding pigeons in a city square. Included in the envelope dated April 25, 1940, are pictures of the *USS Maryland* firing rounds and the *USS Wasp*. The stamp is clipped from the envelope, perhaps by a collector over the years.

On December 18, 1942, Ivah Ree received her last card from Goldman. "A Merry Christmas to the Pal O' my Heart."

The "Pal O' my Heart" is a song written in 1923 by Jesse Crawford, with music and lyrics by Benny Davis.

Many versions of that sentimental song were written in poems during the 1930s. The poem inside Goldman's card reads:

> I like to think of you, my own
> As the dearest pal I've ever known,
> A jolly pal when I feel glad,
> A cheery pal when I am sad,
> A helpful pal come good or bad,
> A loyal pal—and let me add—
> The best good pal one ever had,
> And year by year you grow more near,
> For you are the Pal O' My Heart, my dear.

On the back of the card, Goldman wrote:

"Been on the go again. I am now stationed at the below address for the duration."

Repair Division Section Base
　　Little Creek, Virginia

The Economics of War and How We Got There

In the late 1930s, while Ivah Ree was fresh out of high school and living with her family in rural Georgia, national and international events were setting the stage for her eventual decision to enlist in the WAVES.

America was recovering from the Great Depression and taking a hands-off approach to the war in Europe. The Axis countries of Germany, Italy, and Japan were building an arsenal of planes, tanks, ships, and bombs to exceed the firepower of the allied countries of Britain, France, and the United States. British Prime Minister Winston Churchill pleaded for help against the Nazi aggression. Going against the isolationists at home who did not want to send American soldiers into the war abroad, President Roosevelt instituted America's first peacetime military draft in October 1940.

Roosevelt stepped up his non-military commitment to the war effort abroad in his famous Arsenal of Democracy Speech delivered to the American people on the radio:

> "Guns, planes, and ships have to be built in the factories and arsenals of America… But all our present efforts are not enough. We must have more ships, more guns, more planes—more of everything. This can only be accomplished if we discard the notion of 'business as usual' … We have furnished the British great material support, and we will furnish far more in the future."

Taking the middle ground, The Lend Lease plan would supply Britain with equipment of war, if not the soldiers.

After the attack on Pearl Harbor in 1941, industrial plants signed contracts with the government to manufacture various types of war machinery, converting their facilities to war production. Because this created a labor shortage, advertisements for women workers soon appeared.

Blue-collar women already in the labor force in 1940 were the first to go to work in the factories. Many women were happy for the opportunity of an industrial job that paid $37 a week compared to that of a waitress at $14 a week. Many laundries and restaurants closed during the war because their owners could not keep workers at the wages they paid. White women and Black women left cleaning jobs for factory work.

At that time, textile mills and apparel manufacturing were the dominant industries and main employers for local residents. The city of Winder, Georgia, was once known as the "Working Clothing Capital of the World."

For many young women in Monroe, Georgia, where Ivah Ree grew up, Barrow Manufacturing, 'the pants plant', as it was known, offered a steady income just a ten-minute drive away. The company may have launched a line of military uniforms or other military items.

To pay off her car, Ivah Ree worked in the plant for six years after high school and then left to join the WAVES.

One of seven children, Ivah Ree lived with her parents in rural Monroe, Georgia. They were farmers, and she was a factory worker. Ivah Ree was good friends with Julia Coker, who also worked at Barrow Manufacturing. The plant opened in 1931, so it was new when Ivah Ree and Julia started sewing there in 1936.

After the World Trade Agreement in 1995, many plants were shuttered and businesses moved off shore. Barrow Manufacturing survived until 2006. Julia Coker rose through the ranks as a blue-collar worker. She enjoyed a long career there and went on to become a manager. She also was instrumental in opening a plant in Haiti. Julia Coker was also my father Dan Coker's sister. Ivah Ree spent much of her free time visiting with Aunt Julia. That is how she met my father.

"I grew up with that family," Mother said in my interview of her many years later.

Ivah Ree dated Dan Coker before the war, but as his younger sister Annette said, "They were not serious until after the war."

In my interview with Mother, I asked where she was when Pearl Harbor was attacked.

"I was at someone's house, and there was a phone call."

"Whose house?"

"I was at Julia's," she murmured.

It was a Sunday afternoon around 2:00 pm on the east coast with the time change from Honolulu. Maybe they had just finished lunch together, including my dad.

I asked Mother if Dan, my father, was her one true love.

She looked aside. "Well, I had friends." She gave me a coy smile.

Dan Coker, One True Love
(1912-1989)

Dan Coker was Ivah Ree's husband and my father. He was born in 1912, the second oldest in a family of six children. His father, John Russell Coker, died from measles during an epidemic in 1922. Dan dropped out of school at age 10 with a third-grade education to help his mother run the farm. He, along with his older sister Francis, who was 12, managed to keep the household together and take care of the younger siblings, who were John B., age 9, Henry, age 6, and Julia, age 1.

Frederica Coker, (we called her Grandma Fred), Dan's mother, had a rough year; her 2-year-old son Ross died from measles the same year she gave birth to Julia. The next year, her husband John died, too. Soon after that, Frederica was committed to the mental asylum in Milledgeville, for two years with a nervous breakdown. The Georgia State Sanitarium in Milledgeville was one of the largest mental hospitals in the United States.

Uncle Early, who was a blacksmith in Winder, and Uncle Jim, both brothers of John Russell Coker, helped out with the farm and the care of the children. When Grandma Fred returned from Milledgeville, she home-schooled Dan, but she spent the next five years in and out of the sanitarium.

Grandma Fred's brother, Ernest Breedlove, pushed her to marry again, as a single mother of six children with a farm to run. She married Martin Tomlin in 1931, and Annette was born in 1932. The marriage did not last, and she lost the farm during the Depression.

Annette is my father Dan's half-sister and remaining survivor of the family. I interviewed her about their history. I asked how Ivah Ree and Dan met. She wasn't sure, but Ivah Ree was always over at the Cokers' house, she told me. Ivah Ree and Julia were friends, and Dan was Julia's older brother by nine years.

"Do you think they met at a dance?"

"No, Dan didn't like to dance," Annette said.

But I remember dancing with my dad while standing on his feet when I was little. He asked me to dance when I was in high school, and he chaperoned a school prom. He had a great little Fox Trot.

"They probably got together at someone's house party," Annette said.

Mother once told me Dan was falling down drunk when she met him. Maybe that was at a house party in Bethlehem, Georgia, where he lived with Grandma Fred. I found notations in an autograph book about the fun parties in Bethlehem.

That my dad would be a drinking man after being forced to grow up at age 10 is understandable. He was the oldest boy in the family to take care of his mother after his dad died. Maybe it is how he coped.

In this next picture, taken before the war, Dan looks like he's had a drink. Mother seems a bit annoyed and at the same time entertained, given her Mona Lisa smile. Aunt Julia sits with Perry Hugh, Mother's brother, who also served in World War II.

Dan was drafted in 1942, at age 30, two years after President Roosevelt instituted the first peacetime military draft. His brother Henry had enlisted years earlier, and his younger brother John B. married, leaving Dan as the sole provider for the family.

He had cared for his mother since age 10 and continued to live with her and Julia and Annette after Grandma Fred's failed marriage. The family appealed to the draft board because he was the breadwinner, but he shipped out anyway. Dan was gone for three years and never came home on leave, nor did he write to anyone. Despite his worry for his fragile mother and his place as father figure to his younger sisters, he distanced himself from them as a method to survive the war.

"He didn't want to come home on leave and then say goodbye again. It would be too painful," Annette said.

The U.S. National Archives & Records Administration for Dan B. Coker reads:

> Education, 2 years of high school,
> Marital Status, single, with dependents,

Civilian Occupation, Semi-skilled linemen and servicemen, telegraph, telephone, and power.

Dan worked for the Walton Electric Company before the war and returned to that job, when it was known as the REA (Rural Electric Association), part of President Roosevelt's New Deal to employ men returning from the war. It was an easy transition for Dan, since he ran telegraph poles throughout South Africa while he was in the service.

Stationed in Johannesburg, or as he called it, "J-burg," he remembered with fondness the men who served with him, all playing cards and joking about who owned Coney Island when they placed their bets. He talked often about his experiences there until I teased him. "We've heard that story a million times."

"When he came home from the war, he never wanted to leave again," Annette said.

Dan and Ivah Ree were sweethearts before the war and started seeing each other again, when they both returned home in 1945.

"Mama wanted Dan to marry Ivah Ree because at 33 he was getting old," Annette said.

Dan was five years older than Ivah Ree and grew up in the same town. "He just lived down the road," she said.

He married my mother after she said, "How 'bout it?"

I learned after Mother died that Dan never wrote to her while he was away. Afraid he wouldn't come back, he wanted her to find someone else. Coonce, Mother's friend from the WAVES, told me this story when she called me after Mother's funeral.

Dan was drafted in 1942, and Ivah Ree enlisted in 1943, the same year Goldman Frase married.

Which brings us to the question: What happened to Goldman Frase?

He was a career man who enlisted in the Navy in 1932. Ten years older than Ivah Ree (who graduated high school in 1936), Goldman started writing to her in 1937. Ivah Ree wrote to Goldman for five years while dating Dan before the war. Her last card from him was delivered on December 18, 1942.

Since Ivah Ree was in Washington D.C., for the duration of the war, and Goldman was in Little Creek, Virginia, they came in close proximity in 1943. According to Ancestry.com, Goldman married February 21, 1943. Ivah Ree enlisted on August 12, 1943, so when she arrived in Washington D.C., Goldman was already married.

Goldman was released from the Navy in 1954. Maybe Ivah Ree decided she would rather marry a hometown boy than one who moved every few years. She was a country girl and not likely to change even after seeing the big cities of Washington, D.C., and New York. She wanted to go back home. She knew Dan would be there with his family, even though he never wrote to her while he was away.

When they both returned home from the war in 1945, with Grandma Fred's coaxing and Ivah Ree's proposal, Dan accepted. They married in 1946, and my brother Wayne was born in 1947. I was born in 1949, and my sister Valerie was born in 1951. Wayne and I are pictured with our parents.

Dan took care of his family for most of his life. When I was a teenager, I asked him what he was living for.

"To provide for you kids," he said.

Postscript

The history of World War II unfolded for me through the cards and pictures of Goldman Frase, a man I never heard Mother mention. In researching him through Ancestry.com and reading the reports of the attack on Pearl Harbor, I felt I knew him in some small way. The fact that he played football with the officers who died at Pearl Harbor was chilling to me. I took Mother to visit Pearl Harbor when I was a flight attendant for United Airlines and Honolulu was my route. She became tearful as we stood atop the *USS Arizona* memorial.

"Those men are still down there," she said, as the oil bubbled up from the ship still lying on the bottom of the harbor. Perhaps she thought of Goldman. Whether he was a friend or a sweetheart, I will never know, but she saved his Christmas cards all her life, so I know he meant something to her. He was born in McMinn, Tennessee. He married there, and he is buried there.

When I researched my dad's family through Ancestry.com, the story of Grandma Fred emerged. I knew she spent time in Milledgeville, but after I looked at those birth and death dates of all her children and her husband John Russell, I saw another provocative story—the reason for her nervous breakdown.

Grandma Fred recited long poems to entertain us whenever she babysat us. My aunt Annette, who has provided a good history for my story, told me that Grandma Fred was accepted to a college after high school, but her father would not let her attend.

During the war, Grandma Fred worked in the cotton mill. A bus came by the little town of Monroe every day, picking up women, taking them to the cotton mill to work, and then dropping them back home each night. Annette thought Grandma Fred enjoyed her employment and getting out of the house.

While her mother was at work, 10 year-old Annette stayed with Aunt Francis, who had two children by then. Aunt Julia was 20 and working at the pants plant at the time Dan was drafted. Grandma Fred died when I was in high school.

In Mother's pictures, cards, and brochures, I see a different woman than the one I knew when I was growing up. She was resourceful, going to work as soon as high school was out. She was brave, leaving her large family in rural Georgia to join the WAVES and move away from home. During the war, she was adventurous—very different from the housewife she became when she had three children.

Mother's friend Coonce called me after Mother died. She told me that her mother did not want her joining the WAVES because of the class of women who might serve there. They may be poor and uneducated and from criminal families. She went on to say that the women she met in the WAVES were some of the best friends she ever could have made, including Ivah Ree.

Now the smiling faces of the military men and women go back into their box of memories, to the basement where I found them. Their time was World War II, and they served their country well at home and abroad, on the ships based in the Atlantic and the Pacific, and across the landscape of South Africa and Europe. They were young and full of hope and ambition for a better life.

Afterwards they returned home to peacetime and jobs and the cotton fields, but they talked about the horrific war and the uncertainty of those years. The irony is, they missed it.

The 1960s

1960-1964

In the summer, Mother ran a veritable food processing plant in our kitchen. We used all the fruits and vegetables grown on the four acres surrounding our modest brick home. Every day something cooked on the stove or dripped from a bag that hung on a cabinet knob over a catch pan. Black-eyed peas, butter beans, and corn were frozen. Glass jars of tomato soup lined the counter tops, their Ball Dome lids popping when sealed, the final stage of the home canning process. Grapes, apples, and strawberries were cooked and dripped into jellies and jams.

Mother and Aunt Dovie made wine from scuppernong grapes. Grandma's figs and pears turned into sweet preserves. Every year the trees in the front yard dropped pecans that we shelled into one-quart plastic bags and stored in a freezer that took up all the space in the storage room off the kitchen porch.

Mother sat shelling butter beans into a metal basin on her lap while watching a soap opera, never looking at her hands.

"Can we change the channel?"

"No. I'm watching my program. Get outside and play. Don't come back till supper," she said.

We went outside and batted the ball around or rode our bicycles till dinnertime at five o'clock.

Mother cooked the butterbeans and fried a pan of pork chops. She formed biscuits with her hands in a large wooden bread bowl, first sifting the flour, then adding a scoop of Crisco with her fingers. She poured in sweet milk, by her measure, forming a bowl shape into the flour. She mixed the ingredients by hand, squeezing them between her fingers, picking up more flour until a ball formed. Then she pinched a small piece of the ball, rolled it, flattened it to a biscuit shape, and placed it on the bread pan. We had biscuits every night.

"Stir those butter beans for me," she said.

"With what?" I loved to test her patience.

"With your finger." Mother gave me a hard look, then pointed to the back screen door. "Go to the garden and get some scallions."

Mother gave my sister and me the choice to wash dishes or go work in the garden after supper. I'd much rather work in the garden than be in the house cooking or washing dishes.

I ran out the back door, letting the screen slam, and jumped off the small brick porch and the four steps. The garden was just past the pumphouse and the clothesline. Sometimes she asked me to fetch other raw vegetables from the garden like tomatoes, scallions, cantaloupe, or watermelon. We roasted peanuts or boiled them for a snack. If we had a big crop, Jack Queen's Grocery bought the surplus.

Jack and Grace Queen, friends of my parents, owned a grocery store a short distance down Highway 11. As the grocery store grew over the years, they opened Jack Queen's #2 on the edge of town in the Black neighborhood.

My brother Wayne worked at the store, putting up stock, and life seemed easy going and simple in the early '60s, but that would soon change.

In 1962 a prevailing sense of doom washed over the country during the Cuban Missile Crisis. On the news every night, we watched the standoff between President John Kennedy and Premier Nikita Khrushchev over the Russian build-up of missiles, ninety miles off our shore. Kennedy gave a deadline to dismantle or go to war. In the countdown of those days, America grew more anxious. We went about our business with a heightened sense of impending ruin.

Aunt Dovie had built a bomb shelter—a closet stocked with canned goods, water, a transistor radio, and batteries. Some people converted their root cellars into shelters. At Walker Park Elementary, we practiced getting under our desk during a bomb scare. In the cities, the yellow triangle logo marked concrete fallout shelters.

Khrushchev let every day tick by until the deadline passed. Schools turned out early, and anxious bus drivers hurried everyone home. We huddled around the television for the six o'clock news with Walter Cronkite.

My dad sat leaning on one end of the green vinyl couch with his feet up. Mother sat on the other end with her legs folded beside her. No one wanted to sit between them because they farted loudly all night long, so my brother Wayne, my sister Valerie, and I sprawled on the wood floor, shoulder touching shoulder, waiting for the news.

When Wayne threw his arm around my neck, the wrestling began. Valerie might get kicked as we bonked each other's head on the floor, laughing at the noise. Often, Valerie took off, sliding in her sock feet, crashing us into the chair that banged into the wall, leaving a dent. We wrestled with pent up energy left over from a day at school, as our parents watched, passive yet anxious.

"Quiet," Dad barked. "The news is on."

The large TV inhabited a cabinet piece of furniture in the living room. Its circular handles swung the wood doors open. Walter Cronkite stared back at us through the Sylvania picture tube. The base of the TV housed the large speaker covered by a heavy fabric to enhance the sound. One round knob controlled the on/off switch and the volume while the knob on the opposite side of the cabinet changed the three channels.

"The crisis is over. Cuba is dismantling the missiles," Cronkite said.

"The Kremlin said JFK was a paper tiger," Cronkite continued, " 'But the tiger has teeth,' was Khrushchev's reply.' "

The next year President Kennedy was assassinated.

I sat in an eighth grade math class when the principal made the announcement over the intercom. "President Kennedy has been shot."

Big Don Watkins turned in his seat and called out, "Good, I hope he dies."

The next announcement came soon after. "The President of the United States has died."

"He deserved it," Don said.

That was my first introduction to politics.

I stared at the television as Lyndon Baines Johnson was sworn into office on an airplane with blood-splattered, First Lady Jacqueline Kennedy by his side. Then a few days later I couldn't take my eyes off the funeral procession, those two small children watching their father's horse-drawn caisson, little John John's impromptu salute, and Jackie's kiss goodbye to the flag-draped coffin—images burned in my memory forever.

Meanwhile, racial integration stirred angry debate. Lester Maddox wielded an axe handle and threatened to bash Black heads who tried to integrate his restaurant. He would go on to become governor of Georgia. Martin Luther King, Jr., marched on Washington with Attorney General Bobby Kennedy at his side. King made fiery speeches about equality and overcoming oppression. The crowds loved him.

As a Baptist minister from Atlanta, he organized peaceful marches and advocated nonviolence. He headed the Southern Christian Leadership Conference and was pivotal in ending legal segregation of African American citizens, as well as creating the Civil Rights Act of 1964 and the Voting Rights Act of 1965. King received the Nobel Peace Prize in 1964.

In 1968 while preparing for a march in Memphis, Tennessee, as he stood on the balcony of the Lorraine Motel with his associates, he was assassinated. No one was surprised, not even King, but the country mourned the passing of the fearless civil rights leader.

We were shaken by the violence, a country in revolt, but time went on. The marches continued, and the police used billy clubs to disperse the crowds. On the news every night there were beatings and blastings of Black people with water hoses. It seemed far away in the cities, certainly not on Highway 11. Here, the Blacks kept to themselves except maybe to sell moonshine or clean someone's house.

When Bobby Kennedy died by an assassin's bullet two months later, my mother became distraught and afraid. "This has got to stop!" she cried. "What is happening to this country?"

Only thirteen years old, I really didn't understand, but the messages were powerful. A new fear washed over the country: "What to do about the Black folks?" They were on the rise, and white people were afraid of them.

The Civil Rights Act of 1964 ordered that all schools and public places desegregate. Rather than integrate, city pools closed because no one wanted to swim with the Black kids.

I swam in our city pool a few times before it closed. A huge pool with a diving board, concession stand, and large bathrooms with showers now stood closed to the public. All the white kids felt punished along with the Black kids with no place to swim.

Superintendent of Schools Clyde Pearce built the first backyard pool in the county during integration. My brother and his friends who lived in the county helped build the pool for Mr. Pearce, so we all felt entitled to it and had an open invitation to come swim. There was no such alternative for the Black kids.

A powerful man, Clyde Pearce, who also was President of the Mountain Creek Baptist Church congregation, led the vote on what to do if a Black family wanted to come to our church. As God-fearing Christians, we voted to let them in, but they never came. The members of the Black community of Monroe were reluctant integrationists. They preferred to keep to themselves and lead anonymous, undramatic lives. They wanted little interaction with the white man except maybe to sell him liquor.

The integration of Monroe High School was a careful process. Under the direction of Clyde Pearce, three Black students were hand-selected for this awful duty. They were the smartest, and most likely to succeed in a hostile environment.

Precious Jackson, Dorcus Winters, and Castille Alcott, the lone boy, entered the all-white Monroe High School in 1964. They looked like scared rabbits, waiting for the first shout of the n-word or the slug of a fist.

Most of the white kids felt sorry for their predicament and tried to give them peace if not acceptance.

One loudmouth, David Johnson, shouted in Castille's face, "You have ruined my senior year!"

It was also my brother's senior year.

Castille, who was taller, stared him down, waiting. David backed off.

Precious's eyes fixed on her books as she sat in my tenth-grade classroom. She wore a plaid shirt waist dress with pleats ironed to perfection. The cream in her hair straightened it to the popular bubble style. Everyone watched her, trying to get her attention, but she sat without saying a word. The occasional spit ball landed on her desk. She ignored it.

The teacher called out her name.

"Here," she said in a deep voice.

Everyone laughed. The next day she didn't answer the roll. The teacher knew she was there. We all knew she was there. Not everyone was hostile to her, but everyone was curious.

Anne Bishop, the class clown, was the first to engage her. When the teacher wasn't in the room, she talked to Precious out loud to entertain everyone.

"Precious, what are you doing?"

"Can I borrow your comb?"

"Precious, you forgot to shave your legs last night."

One day Anne pulled black fuzz off the sweater in front of her and stuck it to the armpit of her own yellow cardigan so it looked like hair. She raised her arm and turned to Precious. "Precious, this is what your armpit looks like." She pointed with her # 2 yellow pencil.

Smiling, teasing, we watched Precious' reaction. She sat stony faced for a few seconds, then cracked into a laugh. We made our first Black connection. We all laughed as Mrs. Robinson strolled back into the classroom.

Ol' Lady Robinson was a real tough bird. She wore spiked heels, slim skirts with fitted jackets, red lipstick, and tight curls. She had a pointed nose, eyeglasses with pointed frames, her shoes had pointed toes, and her red fingernails were filed to point.

Tall in her seat, she could see everyone from her chair. One look from her, and we were busted. Other teachers we reduced to a frustration of tears, but not Mrs. Robinson. She stopped us with a word or a look.

On a Monday morning Mrs. Robinson called out our scores for the six-week period, asking if anyone disagreed with their grade. She had given me an eighty-eight. I knew I had not made below a ninety, so I raised my hand. She looked at me through her pointy glasses.

"What do you think your grade should be?" Her eyes pierced mine.

I squirmed, wondering if I had made a mistake and why I now raised my hand. "Higher?" I squeaked.

She arched her pointy eyebrows and added my scores. "You're right! Ninety-two."

Whew, what a relief.

Our assignment that day was to recite, in front of the class, the preamble to the Gettysburg address.

When it was Precious' turn to go, she stood there looking out to the sea of white faces, some angry, some waiting for her to make a mistake so they could laugh. Standing there for a few seconds, she took a breath and opened her mouth. We waited, but no words came out. She lowered her head and cried. I wanted to cry, too.

Mrs. Robinson sprang to her side and hugged her. She walked Precious back to her seat, whispering to her. No one made a sound as we realized the huge responsibility on the shoulders of that young girl chosen to integrate our school.

"Four score and seven years ago, our fathers brought forth to this land a new nation conceived in liberty and dedicated to the proposition that all men are created equal."

It was a powerful lesson in history class that day.

Old Cars

When I was growing up, my parents owned some really cool cars. Our 1939 rag-top Buick Roadmaster looked like a bootlegger's car, one Al Capone might have driven. We saw the road moving beneath us through the rusted-out floorboard. Wayne, Valerie, and I stuck our heads through the holes in the roof of the car as we stood on the back seat. Dad drove down the street with three little heads popping out.

Many years later, our 1956 green-and-white Ford Fairlane often broke down, stranding us on the highway.

"Oh me, I hate this old car," Mother said.

At the REA company picnic, she whined, "We have the oldest car here."

While driving home later that day, Dad thumped his cigarette out the window, but it flew back into the car. Overnight, it smoldered and burned out the entire back seat. Dad pulled out the cushions, and we rode back there on the metal frame with the pungent odor of smoke for months. We smelled like burnt car everywhere we went before he found mismatched seats at a junk yard.

My dad taught me to drive our 1959 Robin's-egg-blue Plymouth Fury with big fins and push-button controls. Sometimes the buttons would push all the way through the dash board, and I would be stuck in gear. Dad kept a screwdriver handy so he could poke through the open hole and change gears. We drove in circles in the yard around the house before he let me on the street with it.

One Sunday as I drove out of the church parking lot, the preacher's son darted in front me. I hit the brakes, but the pedal slid straight to the floor, only slowing the car enough for the little boy to get past.

"Why didn't you stop, Judy?" Dad said.

"I tried. I don't think the brakes work."

He fixed the brakes, but I avoided that car for a long time.

Wayne's first car was a black, four-speed 1955 Plymouth Belvedere with red, rolled-and-pleated leather interior. He let me drive it one Sunday afternoon for the traditional cruise around the Brazier Burger.

At the Brazier, everyone backed into their parking spaces so they could face the drive-through and watch the parade of '50s and '60s muscle cars revving their V-8 engines and glass-packed mufflers. I was cool on my first go around, but on my next turn, the car stopped in the middle of the drive. I couldn't get it cranked and stalled there, blocking traffic. Wayne sat with a friend parked in another car. He jumped out and ran over. "Get out."

When I climbed out, he slid into the driver's seat, started the Plymouth, and drove off, leaving me stranded there. I glanced around at the sea of cars, wondering what to do. Then, with a purpose, I marched to the window and pretended to order a hamburger, till Wayne came back.

His next car, a white 1962 Chevy Nova, had no radio. For Christmas that year, my parents ordered one from a catalog to surprise him, but it didn't arrive till the spring.

Cousin Jimmy came over that afternoon. "What'd you get for Christmas?" he said to Wayne.

"Nothing," Wayne said.

"Nothing?"

"Well, I got socks and underwear."

"Lemme see 'em."

Wayne opened his dresser drawer and pulled out a pair of socks.

"Those are nice." Jimmy laughed.

Ronnie McDaniel's 1956 Pontiac convertible was the scene of a fond summer memory during my senior year in high school. On a double date, we rode around the Brazier as I lay, sunning myself on the back seat, with my head in my boyfriend David's lap and my feet draped out the other side, since there were no seatbelts. Mother allowed Valerie and me to date our boyfriends on Sunday, in either the afternoon or the evening, but not both. Valerie chose evenings. I preferred Sunday afternoons, especially in the summer, because I loved being outdoors.

That same year, for the prom we decorated the American Legion hall.

David met me there to help. He drove a brand-new, yellow 1967 Ford Galaxy with black leather interior. After a few hours of creating roses out of tissue, it was time to go.

"Meet me at the Brazier." He took off.

I hopped into the Plymouth Belvedere, but it wouldn't start. I sat there for a long time before David came back looking for me.

"What happened?"

"The car won't start."

"Get in. I'll take you home."

At nineteen, I carpooled to work in Atlanta and saved enough money for a down payment on a car. Dad co-signed the note with me so I could buy a brand-new, canary-yellow 1968 MGB with black leather interior. It was the first new car in the family. I remember the scene at the dealership when my parents sat beside me to purchase the car.

"Dan has to be responsible for everything. Cain't she sign for herself and keep us out of it?" Mother said.

The dealer pushed the paperwork in front of Dad. "Sorry, she has to be twenty-one."

I thought Mother had killed the deal. She was the punisher, the disciplinarian, the one who cut the blood out of your legs with a switch, the one who said, "You cain't go, you cain't have it, we cain't afford it."

My dad spoke up. "I'm signing the papers."

"You have delusions of grandeur," Mother said, annoyed that I bought such an extravagant car.

She was probably right.

In my yellow MGB, with the top down, I drove to look at an apartment in Atlanta. I stopped at a red light and someone called my name. I looked over at the car next to me. A pretty Black girl smiled at me with big white teeth.

"Hi, who are you?" I said.

"Precious."

"Oh, hi, Precious. It's good to see you."

"You, too, Judy." She drove off.

She had been in my graduating class.

Like Precious on the day I met her, the first day of integration at our high school, I was starting a new chapter. I moved into a new apartment, in a new city, with new roommates. My life changed overnight, and I hung on for the adventure with some of the characters in Atlanta for the Age of Aquarius, in 1969.

Atlanta and the Age of Aquarius

1969-1970

Hip and cool, Angela was from New York. She had just transferred from NYU to Georgia State University. She wore bell-bottom-pants with Indian print madras shirts, a popular style. With a clothes iron, she straightened her long hair with bangs, like most of us did. She was both street smart and book smart. She ran the show, and we followed.

Barbara, a hairdresser from Covington, a small town outside Atlanta, was a little country girl with big brown eyes.

Sandy, from Monroe, moved in with me, too. My roommates and I went out every weekend to parties hosted by the large apartment complexes. With live bands and a cash bar, The Le Mans Apartment was the place to be for those who trusted no one over thirty.

Tall and stocky Arthur Johnson was a regular at the parties, but he danced to slow songs only. We dated a few times. In his apartment one night, he opened the frosted-over freezer in his refrigerator and pulled out two ice trays. He ran them under hot water in the sink, slammed them on the yellow Formica countertop, and cracked them open by their handles with his large hands. He filled a tall, yellow tumbler to the brim with ice and grabbed the handle of Stole′ Vodka, and poured a generous amount into the ice. Then he popped open the yellow can of tonic and topped it off. He sliced the lime into quarters and twisted one over the large glass.

"Want one?"

"Yes."

He was quite the mixologist.

We sat on the couch, while my roommate, Sandy, and Arthur's roommate, Paul, sat in chairs pulled from the kitchen table. Arthur worked in retail so he could afford a nice apartment. The yellow shag carpet matched the color scheme throughout the room. Even the walls were yellow. In the '60s, that yellow color, or avocado green, was the popular choice in décor; even the appliances came in those colors.

After a few drinks, Arthur grabbed me, turned me over his knee, and spanked me hard.

"Stop, you're hurting me."

"Don't you like that?"

"No, I don't. What's wrong with you?"

"I thought you'd like it."

"Jesus, I would like to go home."

"Okay. Don't get so excited. I'm making another drink, then we'll leave."

He went back to the kitchen with its linoleum floor, now splashed with liquor, and made another Vodka Tonic. Arthur always had a tall vodka in the cup-holder of his Grand Torino.

The four of us piled into his car and drove onto the freeway. A car behind us brightened his lights, indicating for Arthur to move out of the left lane. He grabbed an AK-47 rifle from under his seat with his left hand, held it out the window, and fired off three rounds into the air.

"Thff! Thff! Thff!"

"Take that, motherfucker," he said. "Don't mess with me."

The car backed off. Then gunshots came from behind us.

"Get down. He's got a gun!"

Arthur pushed me to the floor. All I could see in the dark were his feet stomping first the accelerator, then the brakes. He swerved the steering wheel to the left, then the right, trying to pass the car in front of us.

Thump! Thump! Thump!

"Damn, he hit my car!"

Sandy and Paul dived to the floor of the back seat. I bounced below the steering wheel, bruising my back with the door handle, trying not to roll onto Arthur's feet and disturb their work. We flew down the I-75 freeway outside Atlanta at one hundred mph, an easy target for the car behind us.

"Shit! Hang on." Arthur passed a Mustang and exited the freeway on two wheels.

The chasing car followed. All at once, we reached a dead end.

"Oh, fuck! Get out. Head for the woods."

The three of us scurried into the brush while Arthur shut off all the lights and stood behind the car, his gun trained on the road, military-style. He waited a long time. The car didn't come.

"Holy shit," he shouted. "That was wild. You can come out now. He's not coming."

We tiptoed back to the car.

"Ohhhhhhh Shit!!!" Arthur laughed.

He shined a flashlight on the lid of the trunk: three bullet holes. Two inches higher, and one of us would have been hit.

"Are those bullet holes?" Sandy poked her fingers in them.

"Yes, they are. Get in."

"They're still warm," she said.

We entered the freeway, taking care to look for our pursuers.

Arthur had collected all manner of weapons, some illegal, in his apartment. I had no idea he kept one in his car. As an army reservist, Arthur knew how to use a gun, and it was easy to smuggle them through his military contacts.

The next day in the weight room at the Le Mans Apartments, Barry Hicks, with his blond hair and big blue eyes, bulked up along with the ex-football players and other muscle men. These hard bodies also came to the dance parties, most of the time with petite blonds on their arms.

Weightlifters shined with sweat, and a sour smell filled the gym. We tried to stay out of the way while the clanging weights hit the floor as we watched Barry clean-and-jerk two hundred fifty pounds. He was good looking, and we all wanted to date him. He played hard to get, until Angela introduced us to pot. Then he became everybody's boyfriend.

"Would you like some tea?" Angela gazed at me with big green eyes.

"No thanks," I said. "Not much of a tea drinker."

Barbara, Sandy, and Angela left in Barry's car.

Tea was the code name for pot, I learned. Soon, all our friends were having tea. We stopped going to the Le Mans dances, and instead went to

Piedmont Park to hear the new acid rock sound.

The park, a gathering place for people and events, offered two entrances because it surrounded a large lake. Rock bands played there on hot summer nights. Hippies threw Frisbees and sold dope during weekends.

Barry, the bodybuilder from the gym, got involved in the drug market. He dropped out of The University of Georgia, with one quarter left to graduate, to grow and sell marijuana. His hair grew long, and he stopped working out. He offered me a ride downtown in his old car.

"Buckle up, Judy, and don't lean on that door. It won't stay closed."

He skidded the old Ford through an intersection with a hard left turn, pushing me against the passenger door with his outstretched hand. It flew open, and I fell over hanging onto the seatbelt for dear life. My head hung below the open door, so I could see the underside of the car and the street spinning beneath me. Pedestrians on the corners of the intersection shouted in horror.

Barry held me and pushed me at the same time, laughing. When we made the turn, he pulled me back inside, and the door slammed shut. "Judy, you're funny. I wouldn't let you fall."

I laughed too, because I survived. Barry was still strong, even though he stopped lifting weights when he started smoking dope.

The Vietnam War Protest

1969-1972

In 1969 the draft was in place and every eighteen-year-old male had a lottery number. If your number was high, you might not have to go. My brother's number was two. After his four-year college deferment, Wayne shipped out. Mother was sad. She and her brothers, as well as Dad and his brothers, all served in World War II. But she did not want her boy to go to war.

Myopic and slight of build, Wayne was not a fighter. The best student in his class, he earned awards for his brilliance. I remember dancing with him in high school, swinging him around polka style and lifting him off the floor because I weighed more. It was hard to imagine him as a soldier.

I didn't know that much about the war until, as a student at Georgia State University in Atlanta, I read *The Great Speckled Bird*. Founded by activists from Emory University, the counterculture underground newspaper advocated the student war protests that spread across the country. Along with The Students for a Democratic Society (SDS), who were active on campus in their quest for equality, economic justice, and peace, my roommate Sandy and I attended student sit-ins at Emory University.

The students presented their arguments. "The U.S. is on overkill with too much technology against people living in the jungle. Why are we there? We can't police the world. If the Communists want it, let them have it. It's a jungle."

Vietnam was too far away and no threat, except to the young boys who were forced to serve in the unpopular war. Some fled to Canada. My brother was in Cambodia because he was drafted, and I became a war protester.

Tear gas filled the air in Piedmont Park. With the exits blocked off, hippies were arrested. We outnumbered the police and began to overtake their cars, climbing on them and stopping them in their tracks. We rescued a young boy in the backseat by shaking the car till the door flew open. Another paddy wagon came through with Mayor Sam Massell's wife, who was arrested as a war protester. We hippies repeated that rumor because we thought it gave us political clout.

Police swarmed Piedmont Park, herding us from one end of the park to the other. The air nauseated me. An Eastern Airlines stewardess in our group panicked, looking for a way out. She would lose her job if she went to jail. We were stranded with no food or water and the thick smell of mace. Many hours passed before the raid ended, and the crowd dispersed. None of my friends was arrested that day, although some of them were draft dodgers.

Our friend Barry was among them. Always a free thinker, he ran around bare-foot, even in the winter because he had no money. He sold his blood to pay rent on a large house with six other guys. To avoid the draft, he asked me to break his foot by running over it with his car. I couldn't do it, so his roommate did.

He got drunk and stoned so he couldn't feel it. When that didn't work, he ran up and down stairs to elevate his blood pressure before his interview with the recruiter. When that didn't work, he became a draft dodger.

Another friend, David Sword, was AWOL when he was shot in a drug deal in Canada. His girlfriend Ann left Atlanta to bring him home. She had no "bread" or car, so we all chipped in and bought a pound of grass for her to sell and finance her trip up the coast. She was six months pregnant.

A more famous war protester, Muhammad Ali, made the conscientious objector claim a popular one. He was stripped of his heavyweight championship for two years while he fought the Supreme Court for his right as an Islamist whose religion prohibited him from going to war. He would have gone to jail for not reporting for duty, but the Court ruled in his favor. When he returned to the ring, his first contest was in Atlanta against Jerry Quarry. We watched it on closed-circuit TV. Ali was a folk hero of the hippies.

The war had gone on too long, and the people at home became hostile toward the military industrial complex. The My Lai Massacre of villagers, including women and children, perpetrated by Lt. William Calley; the near-genocide air-bombing raids on peasants with small arms; the four dead in Ohio at Kent State University campus, where student demonstrators were shot down by the National Guard, now infuriated the country.

When I think of the four dead at Kent State University, I am angered all over again, remembering how the United States gunned down their own citizens on a college campus.

My brother served as a medic in Cambodia and came home on leave. He fell asleep on my couch. When I tried to wake him and offer him a bed upstairs, he was startled and threw me to the floor. Lesson learned: Never wake a soldier from his slumber. You might get hurt.

Wayne could sleep standing up, something he learned in Vietnam. He came home shell-shocked and jumpy. He didn't want to go out to crowded or unfamiliar places.

He saw a lot of horror as a medic, but we never talked about the war. He didn't want to. He came home on leave, and my apartment was full of people and music, so we had little time to converse. Even when I drove him to the airport, we talked of small things. Like many servicemen, he just wanted to forget. Wayne was never the same after Vietnam. None of us was.

We were the flower children and as the Beatles' "Revolution" sang, "We all want to change the world."

"Peace, Love, and Rock and Roll" became our mantra. Fueled by marijuana and music, we were the revolutionaries, and like most revolts, it started on the college campus, where intellectuals had time to consider the real problems and effect change. Our numbers were large, and we were united in one cause, all across the country—"Stop the war."

Soldiers in uniform returning from Vietnam were surprised to be called "baby killers" by U.S. citizens. They did not get the welcome most enlisted men before them received. The war's unpopularity increased at home, and in some demonstrations, the public saw the military as an enemy of peace and spit upon them. War protests and riots ripped through every campus. Soon businesses and the general population demanded an end to the military supremacy effort in Vietnam.

My brother did not wear his uniform when he came home after two years, but everyone recognized his class-A haircut. He bought gifts for our family. For himself he bought a reel-to-reel Teac tape system, very desirable then and a collector's item today. Very soon it was stolen from his trailer in Athens, Georgia. He was living hand-to-mouth, like most of us kids were.

Along with giant, hand-carved, wooden spoons and a clay water pot from Vietnam, Wayne also brought home some strong weed.

Drugs were plentiful in Vietnam. Some of the marijuana the servicemen brought back was so heavy in effect, the paranoia it produced was frightening. I smoked some once and could not function. I panicked and none of my friends could comfort me during those terrible few hours. Afterwards I steered clear of that medicine.

Many of my friends did LSD, mescaline, and mushrooms. I was afraid of hallucinogens. I only did black beauties (speed) once to study for a French final, on which I made an A.

With the drug culture came great music. In Piedmont Park we listened to The Allman Brothers Band. They had just played the Fillmore East, and with two drummers, Southern Rock was born.

Some of the best music of the day were war protest songs. Country Joe and the Fish wrote "The Fish Cheer," a rollicking song about Vietnam and how you can be the first one on your block to have your boy come home in a box.

Crosby, Stills, and Nash wrote "Four Dead in Ohio," a mournful harmony about the "tin soldiers and Nixon coming" and gunning down war protestors at Kent State. One chilling lyric asks, "How would you feel if you found her dead on the ground?"

Along with great music in the park, hippies set up food stations for all to partake. In 1970 the macrobiotic diet was popular. It looked like "brown rice, seaweed, and a dirty hot dog" (as described by Bob Dylan in "On the Road Again"). It was not very appetizing fare, but the hippies swore by it.

The importance of yin and yang in your life and diet and the need for oriental-style balance was described in "You Are All *Sanpaku*," a popular book of the day. It was a study of how your body can give you signs of *sanpaku*, or being out of balance. If there were a white space between the iris of your eye and your eyelids, then you were *sanpaku*. You were advised to eat more brown rice or something, if you subscribed to this thinking. We steered clear of that thinking and the diet at the park as well.

I was part of a movement to change the world at every level, including personal and physical. No more working only for the almighty American dollar, but also to make a difference in the lives of people. We had a better way, a revolution of culture. Not exactly sure what to change, but the status quo could not be tolerated. Anything antiestablishment inspired us.

My roommates and I took our Frisbees to hang out at Piedmont Park. Four of us lived in a two-bedroom apartment in the Buckhead neighborhood in Atlanta. Then Connie moved in and slept on the couch.

She was beautiful with bee-stung lips, clear blue eyes, and honey-colored hair that cascaded into soft, thick curls at her shoulders. Her skin was flawless with the palest rosy blush on her cheeks. She suntanned before the rest of us. What a backdrop for those lips and eyes. If Helen's was the face that launched a thousand ships, then she looked like Connie. She met and fell in love with John Roscoe, son of a famous Atlanta lawyer.

John's mother owned an elegant mansion on West Paces Ferry Road. With our gang of friends, we hung out there sometimes. I remember sitting on Mrs. Roscoe's lovely kitchen countertop, swinging my bare feet, when she gave me a look that sent me to the floor to stand like a lady.

My roommates and I were just kids crowded into a small apartment. John and a group of friends including Ben Farber, Barry, Bill Brooks, and others rented an antebellum house downtown that was sparsely furnished. We hung out there, too.

"Do you want to ball?" John said to me first.

"No."

He then asked my roommate Sandy, and they went upstairs to have sex in one of the bedrooms.

Sex was casual with some of my friends, but I was much more reserved. No one took birth control, and condoms were used sparingly. I had sex a couple of times and was on pins and needles until my period. The last thing I needed was to get pregnant. The guys called me a "cold fish." Some of my friends had abortions. David, who was AWOL, and his girlfriend Ann had their baby out of wedlock.

Connie was pregnant when she married John. It was a big wedding, and all of us roommates were bridesmaids, dressed in long, brown satin gowns. To Connie's dismay, I wore boots with my dress instead of heels, but I had little money to spend.

"Why is it no adults will talk to me?" our friend Allen Rabin said to the preacher at Connie's wedding reception. "No one takes me seriously. Why is that?"

The preacher looked at him and then searched for an exit. "Maybe you should cut your hair," he said, and scurried out of the room.

"Did you see that? He's afraid of me, too," Allen whined.

"Allen, did you think because he is a preacher he would talk to you?" I said.

Allen was a short little hippie with long hair. Before he started smoking dope and eating macrobiotic food, he was a bodybuilder. He came from a wealthy Atlanta family, but he swore there was a better way of life. The last time we saw him was in the hospital with his mother at his bedside. He was green with hepatitis —too much macrobiotic food. In the years that followed, we lost track of many characters in our gang, including Allen.

John was older than most of us. He was short, stocky, and well-dressed. He owned many cars. He also had a Harley Davidson motorcycle that he ripped up and down the streets of West Paces.

He rode his bike one afternoon with a roll of cash in his hip pocket. The road was under construction, and he bounced through a pothole. The cash came floating out into the air. Workers on the street scrambled to collect the money. He realized the road crew was picking up hundreds of dollars of his money, and he kept going. That is the image I have of John Roscoe. Money is flying out his ass, and he doesn't look back.

We took turns racing through the winding streets of Chastain Park on the back of John's Harley. My yellow MGB, now a little faded from a wreck, chased after. We loaded into John's van to go to concerts. Mattresses, pallets, and psychedelic posters took the place of the back seat. The stereo blasted "Lucy in the Sky with Diamonds," "Guinevere," and "White Bird." We got tickets to see Black Sabbath in Chastain Park and The Rolling Stones at Auburn University with Chuck Berry as the opening act.

At the Birdcage in downtown Atlanta, Percy Sledge played. It was an all-Black nightclub, but they let the long-hairs in. In those turbulent years of integration and war protests, we were all getting hosed and sprayed with mace, so there was an unspoken bond. All of us wanted to be in the presence of great music.

Janis Joplin played Georgia Tech, Iron Butterfly and Steppenwolf played the Fox. John bought tickets and opened a side door of the Civic Center for the rest of us to see José Feliciano and Santana.

The pop festivals were great gatherings of like-minded people. We found our inspiration in music, and the music found its inspiration in us. It was a lovefest. Sometimes we had to take off our clothes to fully absorb it. Two hundred thousand people attended the Atlanta International Pop Festival of 1969.

I was broke and a friend bought a ticket for me. He wanted to be my sweetheart and my date, but he wasn't my type, so I took the ticket and got into my roommate Sandy's car. The traffic snaked to the event, which was twenty miles outside Atlanta on that hot Fourth of July weekend. Kids sat on the backs of convertibles, trucks, and car bumpers. Some walked as we got closer. We had no idea what to expect.

The moment we arrived, the car was blocked in. We got out and pushed through the crowd to the staging area, and in fact the gate surrounding the event was torn down by the mob. One cute girl I had seen at the dance clubs, always dressed to the nines, was there in a gorgeous white outfit complete with a wide brim hat. It did not stay white long in that mud field.

That summer of love in 1969 was also the summer before my brother left for Vietnam. I found him passed out on a blanket at the pop festival. He had come with a group of friends from back home, but they left him there, so I stayed with him till he woke up. He was drunk and might get stepped on. As soon as he revived, I took off to find my friends from Atlanta.

Vendors were around, but I had no bread, food, or water. The music was constant, with lesser acts during the day and headliners at night. By the time Janice Joplin came on, it was 4:00 a.m. Canned Heat, Grand Funk Railroad, Joe Cocker, Led Zeppelin, Johnny Winter, Creedence Clearwater Revival, and a host of other greats played in those three days.

It was dusty and one hundred degrees when we found Joe Adams, a friend from back home. He had a campsite with sleeping bags, food, water, a grill, and even a toothbrush, which I used. Thank God we found Joe, or we would have died from hunger.

The next day, fire trucks appeared and hosed everyone down, just to cool us. Water was free. We got naked in the fire hoses, and the mud left behind made a sliding pit. People had sex and didn't care who watched.

Sandy smashed a few fenders, trying to move her car before giving up. People passed out in make-shift Red Cross tents—some overdosed.

"Hey, man, we're driving up to Woodstock next month. Want to go?" my friend, Joe said.

"No thanks," I said, certain I would perish.

Back at the apartment the next night after the festival, I took a shower for the first time in four days. "Is the coast clear?" I called out.

"Hold on," Sandy said. "Okay, coast is clear,"

I ran out of the shower into the bedroom I shared with Sandy. I had a towel around me, and my hair was dripping wet. I closed the door and took off the towel to dry my hair. I bent over so my hair fell forward as I wrapped it in the towel. When I turned around, four guys were sitting on the twin beds they had hidden behind.

"Ahhhhhhh!" I scrambled to cover myself and ran back to the bathroom.

"Jesus, Sandy, I thought you got the guys out," I said, as I peeked out the bathroom door.

Laughing, Farber, Brooks, John, and Barry strolled down the stairs. "Don't be mad, Judy. You have a great figure."

I re-entered the bedroom. "Why did you do that, Sandy?"

"They wanted to. I thought it was funny."

"Great. Thanks a lot. What are we doing tonight anyway?"

"Some of the guys are going to John's to jam. We can go with them if you want. Come down when you get dressed. Your cousin is here."

"My cousin?"

"Yeah, Jimmy."

"Oh shit. I'll be right down."

"Good. He looks like he might kill somebody."

I thought back to my childhood days growing up with Jimmy Harris. Like his father, Uncle Perry Hugh, Jimmy had a mean streak in him. He was a former football player and off-the-charts smart. He could have attended any school in the country, including MIT, but he was a country boy who graduated from Georgia Tech.

Jimmy's face was a permanent frown, much like Perry Hugh's. He looked as if he couldn't believe all the shit going on around him. If someone needed to be straightened out, he was the man to do it. He would take you down.

I hurried downstairs to find him sitting on the couch, frowning. "Jimmy, hey, how you doing?"

"Who are these hippies?" he snapped in a loud voice.

"They're friends."

"Friends? Keep 'em away from me, or I'll have to knock one out." He glanced sidelong at Farber, a slight fellow with long, blond hair.

"Hey, man, let's go over to John's," Farber said, getting the hint.

"Good riddance," Jimmy shouted, as they walked out the door.

"God, settle down. What is your problem?" I said.

"I don't have one, but you do, if these are your friends." He studied me. "I was supposed to meet Wayne here. He said there was a party."

About that time, Wayne walked in. "Hey, man, what's going on?"

"Nothing. Where you been?" Jimmy said.

"I stopped for some food. I was starving. Where is everybody?"

"I just ran off a bunch of long-hairs, if that's who you mean. I ain't hanging out with no lowlifes," Jimmy barked.

"Okay, let's make a drink," Wayne said.

Wayne and Jimmy mixed drinks in the kitchen.

"Nice guy," Sandy said in a wry tone.

"Yeah, he's pretty straight." I sighed.

Jimmy comes from a long line of Harrises, my mother's side of the family, which enjoys a long and distinguished history in my hometown. The William Harris Homestead, circa 1825, is one of the few intact plantations remaining in Georgia.

That country lifestyle was in my rearview mirror now, as I embraced the city and the people who could make a difference in the world.

The Finest-Looking Man I Ever Met

1970-1972

"Go tell that girl I'm in love with her," Bob said.

It was spring quarter in that school year on a hot sweltering day. The sun beat down on my red hair, making it feel even hotter. I held my long strands high to allow the air to cool my neck as I stood on the stone bridge overlooking the fountain in Hurt Park at Georgia State University. I leaned against the concrete half-wall so the mist from the fountain wet my face, and that is when I saw a heavyset, young man wearing a madras shirt come up the stairs toward me. He smiled and waved as if he knew me.

"Hi. I'm George," he said, as he stood next to me and pointed. "See that guy down there sitting on the grass? He just moved here from Texas, and he wants to meet you."

I scanned the students on the lawn below. My eyes stopped at Bob's

Bob, US Army Reserves, 1970

shirtless frame and dark skin, as he pretended to be reading—very attractive. George seemed harmless, as I noticed his blue eyes and blond hair framing his face. He gave me a mischievous smile. "What's your name?"

"Judy," I said, with a grin.

"Come on down, Judy. I'll introduce you to Bob." He stepped back and motioned for me to go ahead of him.

As we strolled down the steps, I watched Bob, who continued to read his book until I stood in front of him. Then his eyes surveyed me from my feet to my face, and he flashed an alluring smile. His black curls glistened in the sunlight. His suntanned, bare chest looked strong. Tall, dark, and handsome—the finest-looking man I had ever met.

George made the introductions and disappeared.

"You have beautiful legs," Bob said. "Please, sit down."

My hot pants provided little coverage from the grass, but I sat down anyway, intrigued. "Texas, huh?"

"That's right. Austin. University of Texas. Did George tell you that?"

"He said you just moved here."

"I told him to tell you I'm in love with you."

"How do you know?" I leaned forward to gaze into his eyes.

"You're beautiful. What's not to love? I've seen you on campus driving your little yellow MGB. You were wearing a bolero hat and a mini dress, showing off your long legs. I saw your red hair and green eyes when I gave you my parking space one day right over there on Courtland Avenue." He pointed.

"Oh yeah. I park there illegally every day." I glanced over at my car.

"Yeah, me, too."

"I throw my parking tickets on the floor of my car. I must have a hundred of them." I laughed.

"Yeah, me, too."

"I think I remember the day you gave me your parking spot. You drive a Volkswagen." I studied his face.

"Yes."

"Why did you move here?"

"I broke up with my girlfriend. Time to move on."

"Why here?"

"My brother lives here. I'm staying with him and his family. What about you?"

"I have two roommates," I said, as I peeked at the clock tower. "It's time for my class, but I can cut it."

"No. Go to your class. I'll be waiting right here when you're done."

Bob was different from my other friends, who would have encouraged me to cut class and go out. He seemed mature and serious—a grown-up. When I came back from my English class an hour later, he was still sitting on the grass, getting sun with his shirt off, reading. When he saw me, he packed up his books, and we strolled off campus over the railroad tracks to Underground Atlanta, a shopping and entertainment district, and Bob started singing and dancing to the *West Side Story* anthem.

"When you're a Jet, you're a Jet all the way, from your first cigarette to your last dyin' day." He pretended to smoke, then thump a cigarette to the ground and stamp it out.

Who is this fabulous boy?

After we returned to campus, he suggested we go to Stone Mountain Park. He opened the door to his beige Volkswagen parked on Courtland Avenue a few spaces from my car. The VW was old but immaculate. At Stone Mountain Lake, he offered me his t-shirt to swim in. "You can change in the car," he said, as he opened the trunk to get a towel.

Squirming out of my shorts and bra, I stripped down to the t-shirt and my panties.

The water felt great on that hot day as we ran splashing and diving. I jumped into his strong arms, and he threw me like a little child into the water. After a few embraces and kisses, he held me at arms-length.

"You have small breasts," he said, looking at my wet t-shirt.

No one had ever told me that before.

Most of my friends described me with big boobs and long legs. Bob saw me in a different way. He was much larger and taller than my friends, and he was a bodybuilder. I was small to him.

After our swim, I sat in the car and slipped off my wet panties and redressed into the shorts and shirt I had worn earlier, while Bob stood behind the open trunk of his Volkswagen and pulled out a dry shirt, keeping on his swim trunks.

"I would like to take you out to a nice dinner but…" he showed me his checkbook, and there was only nine dollars and twenty-one cents.

This gesture would portend my future.

At the International House of Pancakes, I ordered strawberry crepes for dinner, and we talked for hours. By the time we got back to campus to pick up my car, it was late, but my car was still there, parked illegally.

"I wish we could go home together," he said as we stood kissing in the moonlight.

Since he lived with his brother's family, and I had two roommates, the possibility of being alone together was not good, but I would have gone anywhere with him that night. He waited while I got into my car and drove off, then he made a U-turn and went the other way.

Meeting Bob was so exciting, I had to tell someone, so I drove to my old hippie roommate's apartment and rang the bell. I had since moved away from 10th Street, 14th Street, the hippie district, and moved in with two schoolteachers to straighten my lifestyle… it was late, but Sandy was up. She opened the door, gave me a hug, and invited me in.

"You won't believe the really cool guy I met today," I said as I flopped down on the small sofa.

"Help me find this hash." Sandy pointed. "It fell in the carpet right here last night."

We both scoured the shag rug on all fours till we came up with it and smoked and talked about Bob.

On our first date, Bob appeared wearing a Schiaparelli pink shirt, a popular color in 1970, with a dark reddish bow tie. In his black-and-white wingtip, dress shoes, he looked like the Great Gatsby, and he held a bouquet of yellow daisies.

"For you," he said.

I took the beautiful flowers and looked in the kitchen for a container. Didn't one of the schoolteachers have a vase? Instead I found a tall, Tupperware cup I had taken from my mother's house, filled it with water, and arranged the flowers there.

I turned and gazed at him. Bob's handsome features added to the confidence he exuded, and without a doubt, he understood how to make an entrance. I had never been wooed before, and Bob knew what he was doing.

We went out to dinner, and he opened all my doors like a gentleman. I was impressed from the start.

We were inseparable. He took over all our plans for the day. He suggested we walk from campus to Peachtree Street to meet his brother Jerry, a stockbroker at Merrill Lynch.

In that busy, high-rise office, his secretary asked us to be seated while Jerry was in a meeting. The overstuffed, leather chair provided a beautiful view of downtown Atlanta from the giant windows.

Soon a larger version of Bob with a booming voice stepped out to greet us. Jerry was very animated, wearing a gray pin-striped suit and dress shoes. We exchanged introductions, and when he gave me the once over, I wished I had worn something that hid my cleavage.

"What kind of shoes are those?" His eyes stopped at my feet.

I picked up my foot to reveal the bottom, which had no soles. They were brown, leather, barefoot sandals with straps wrapping around the foot.

"What happens if you step on something sharp?" He looked amused.

"I'm careful." I blushed, feeling like a poor little hippie who stood out like a sore thumb in this formal setting.

Jerry laughed and then dismissed us so he could return to work.

On the way back to school, the electricity between Bob and me was so strong he swept me off my feet and into his arms, kissing me and holding me high against his hard body, as he kept walking. I felt tiny and sexy embraced in his muscled physique.

"What's that necklace you're wearing?" I held it in my hand, admiring the delicate gold emblem attached to a heavier gold chain. Most of my men friends didn't wear such an intricate piece of jewelry tucked inside their shirt.

"A Star of David," he said.

"What's that?" I examined it closer.

"The Star of David is the Jewish star. I'm Jewish."

Legs Benowitz

1972-1983

At Georgia State University, Bob and I moved in together. After we had been living together for almost two years, I wanted to get married and had proposed to him on more than one occasion.

"I can't get married. I work part time. I'm still in school. I can barely tie my shoes," he had said.

"I applied for a job as a flight attendant with United Airlines," I told him.

"What? When did you do that?" Bob's eyebrows shot up.

"Three weeks ago. I got a letter today. I start training next month in Chicago."

"Why didn't you tell me about it?" Hurt laced his words.

"I didn't think I would get it. I wanted to wait and tell you if I got hired. I applied to Eastern Airlines and Northwest Orient before I met you, and they turned me down." I shrugged. "Maybe I'm better at interviewing now."

"Or maybe you're a good candidate, now that you have two years of college under your belt." He sat down and studied his palm. "Is this what you want?"

"I think so. You're not ready for marriage. I can't wait around. You might never be ready. This is an opportunity for me to travel and make good money."

"I don't want you to go. Is this job more important to you than me? I love you." He sat for a few minutes without saying anything, then sighed. "If I marry you, will you stay?"

I thought about that question and turned away. "Not now. Not with this job offer on the table." I felt conflicted. "You don't want to marry now."

"I know." He paused, thinking. "I can't."

"It's for the best." I tried to sound convincing.

"What will happen to us?" Bob frowned.

"I don't know. We'll just have to find out." I had changed my mind about marriage. I was ready to travel and see the world.

Three weeks later, Bob drove me to the Atlanta airport, and we sat in the parking lot saying our good-byes.

"I feel like we're getting a divorce, and neither of us wants to," he said.

"I know, but I have to do this."

Bob carried my suitcase inside the Atlanta airport terminal to check in. At the gate for my flight to Chicago, I promised to come home soon. He walked me to my seat in first class which was allowed in 1972, before only ticketed passengers were permitted on planes. I gave him one last kiss and watched him go. He looked back with tears in his eyes.

1972, upon graduating United Airlines flight attendant training uniform designed by Jean Louis

"Goodbye, my love," I said.

When the door closed, the flight attendant offered me a drink and introduced me to another candidate for United Airline's flight attendant training—Rosie from Athens, Georgia, a recent graduate of The University of Georgia. We became roommates during our training in the Chicago suburb of Des Plaines, and after six weeks we chose to live together in Washington, D.C., along with Julie from Virginia.

Washington, D.C.
1972-1973

In 1972 Washington, D.C., would be at the center of a political turning point in history. The Pentagon Papers, written by military analyst and American activist Daniel Ellsberg about the controversial Vietnam War, had been leaked to the *Washington Post*. He would be charged with espionage in 1973. The Watergate scandal was at its height, and President Richard Nixon had just been re-elected by a landslide.

My roommate Rosie attended the Republican National Convention in Miami. She worked as a volunteer flight attendant with a group known as the Nixonaires. During our years in Washington, my roommates and I watched as Rosie's candidate fell from grace.

I saw history unfold in real time.

It was past midnight when I searched for a parking spot at my Saxony Square apartment in Alexandria, Virginia, also known as stew-town because many stewardesses lived in the shadow of Washington National Airport, which later would be renamed Ronald Reagan Washington National Airport.

Nothing was available so I drove down to the lower parking area my roommates and I affectionately called "the pit." Instead of walking around to the front where there were lights, I took the short cut up the dark hill to our building in the back of the complex.

I shivered, imagining it was a good place to get kidnapped by someone hiding behind a tree, but I still took that path with my eyes wide open. I could outrun most people, if given an equal chance.

I opened the door to my three-bedroom apartment and threw my keys onto the kitchen table that my roommate Julie had picked up at a garage sale. It was also where I often sat naked drinking coffee and reading the *Washington Post* that landed on my doorstep every morning.

"Could I have some of that paper?" Julie said as she came around the corner. "And could you get dressed? I don't like you sitting with your bare ass on my chairs."

"Okay, sure." I got up as Julie turned on the TV that perched on a stand with wheels. She adjusted the antenna and Martha Mitchell's face appeared on the news. She was the wife of U.S. Attorney General John Mitchell and close friend of President Richard Nixon. The attorney general was sentenced to prison for crimes during the Watergate scandal, and there was his wife on TV, trying to shift the blame to Nixon. She later was ferried away to a hotel in Newport Beach, California, to silence her.

Political intrigue struck close to home on December 8, 1972, when United Airlines Boeing 737, Flight 553 from Washington, D.C., crashed during an aborted landing at Chicago's Midway Airport. It was a "go around" while approaching the airport, meaning the tower instructed the pilot to stop his descent and go around one more time. There are many reasons for this instruction: poor visibility, weather, crowded skies, or crowded runways.

None of the cockpit flight crew survived to tell their story, and the "A-Stew" (senior flight attendant) working in first class also died. The two flight attendants in coach survived and retired from flying. Of the fifty-five passengers, eighteen survived.

Sometimes I worked Flight 553 to Midway out of D.C. In fact, we taxied past the wreckage for weeks until the investigation was complete and the airplane was removed from the inspection site. It was a grim reminder of what could happen.

I called home from a pay phone at the gate. "Mother, hey. It's me. I just wanted you to know I'm okay."

"I did not think otherwise," she said.

"There was a United Airlines plane crash today at Midway in Chicago. Did you hear?"

"Yes, I did."

"Were you worried?"

"No, not really, but I'm glad you called."

"It could have been me," I muttered.

Upon further research on this crash, I learned that the flight data recorder malfunctioned fourteen minutes before the crash, which presented a mystery to investigators. One of the passengers who perished, in addition to Illinois Congressman George W. Collins, was Dorothy Hunt, the wife of soon-to-be convicted Watergate burglar E. Howard Hunt. The crash occurred at the height of the Watergate scandal, and Dorothy Hunt, a CIA operative, had purchased a two hundred fifty thousand-dollar flight insurance policy shortly before the plane took off. Her purse, recovered from the debris, contained more than ten thousand dollars in cash.

Charles Colson, who served as Special Counsel to President Nixon, claimed the CIA had sabotaged the plane. It ended up as one of the most investigated aviation disasters in history, and the National Transportation Safety Board ultimately concluded (in unmistakable non-layman's terms) that "the probable cause of [the] accident was the captain's failure to exercise positive flight management during the execution of a non-precision approach, which culminated in a critical deterioration of airspeed into the stall regime where level flight could no longer be maintained."

In other words—pilot error, the most common cause for an airplane crash.

Even today when I fly and the airplane is on descent for landing, then without warning starts to climb again, I am nervous because I know we are on a "go around," which is always dangerous. Sometimes the pilot cannot get enough lift or visibility, or other obstacles are in the way, like a row of houses on the edge of the runway. That was the case at Midway. The 737 plowed into five houses.

Another flight from the D.C. area, this one from Washington Dulles International Airport, became a prop for political posing when President Nixon decided he should personify energy conservation. It involved United Airline's nonstop Flight 92, which connected to Flight 93 to the Honolulu International Airport. Flight attendants wore black fitted sweaters and floor-length plaid skirts buttoned up the front. I always had my skirt unbuttoned above the knee, earning the nickname "Legs Benowitz." My girlfriend's husband owned a French restaurant in Virginia and named a breakfast menu item after me, "L'eggs Benowitz." It was spicy.

Flight 92 was a trip I often worked, although I was not on that flight the day President Nixon entered the first-class cabin on December 27, 1973. He wanted to score points with the public by flying commercial and saving 60,000 gallons of fuel used to fly his private jet, Air Force One.

Secret Service provided no security sweep of the aircraft, and The Federal Aviation Administration only learned the President was on board as the DC-10 taxied out to the runway. It was the first trip ever made by a sitting US President on a scheduled airliner. Air traffic had no time to implement their special precautionary procedures, which always must be followed when the President takes to the air lanes.

United Airlines made sure he flew back to Washington, D.C., on a military airplane. They did not want the liability.

Aside from the President, it was not unusual to have a famous politician on board. On a flight from D.C. to Denver to go skiing, my girlfriend Roberta and I used an airline employee pass to sit in first-class when Senator Ted Kennedy boarded. He walked past our seats to the coach cabin and sat with his constituents.

I wrote this note on a napkin: A blond and a redhead would like to buy you a drink in the first class cabin.

I gave the note to our flight attendant with instructions to give it to the senator.

We ogled him through the first-class curtain to see if he would come up. He never did. We waited for him to deplane, and he was gracious as he shook our hands when we introduced ourselves. We were thrilled to meet him. He was very handsome in those days. This was three years after the 'Chappaquiddick' scandal in 1969 had stained his reputation with suspicion of an extramarital affair, but on this day, he kept walking.

Ted Kennedy would go on to become the "Lion of the Senate," with fifty years of service.

On another flight I met a man who also would shape the history of this country.

In the coach cabin one afternoon, I worked a flight with my best friend Karen, who could fit in my pocket—she was so small. A tall, blond, handsome, young Air Force captain in a bomber jacket boarded. His name was Andrew Johnson, and Karen made a beeline for him.

"He's cute," she said, after we took off.

"Go hang out with him. I'll work the flight," I said.

"Are you sure?"

"There are only five people on board. Go."

Those were the days of airline subsidies, before the deregulation that came during the Reagan years. There was no need to drag anyone off kicking and screaming. The flights were often empty.

On approach for landing, Karen came back to me. "I've been talking to him for the whole flight, and he hasn't asked for my number."

"Well, write it on a napkin, stick it in his pocket and say, 'Call me,' " I said.

They were married a few short months later.

In 1972 Andrew flew B-52s and dropped bombs on Vietnam. Over his long career, he became the youngest four-star general in the United States Air Force. In 2003 General Andrew Johnson was in charge of Special Operations, and his troops dropped bunker-bombs in Iraq when Saddam Hussein was pulled from a cave.

Married forty-four years now, Karen credits me. She did not last long as a flight attendant, but she made a good military wife.

I felt lost without Bob when I first moved to D.C. I flew back to Atlanta often. Then I started dating and traveling and got used to life without him. The men I dated in Washington were secret service agents who described themselves as trained killers. Also many scientists and law professors invited me to go out on the town or sailing on Chesapeake Bay.

A lawyer I dated invited me to accompany him to his class reunion at George Washington University Law School, a huge event with multiple classes attending at different locations on campus. Bands played at the many sites around the buildings. My strappy, stiletto sandals sunk into the grass as we strolled the school grounds. The dinner was a more formal affair. My date wore a three-piece suit, and I wore a silk halter-top over matching bell-bottom pants.

During the night my halter-style bra became uncomfortable, and I wanted to take it off at the table. I could easily unhook the strap on one side of the front of the bra and discreetly pull it down the other side of the bra hidden by the blouse, then, with a snap of the thumb and index finger, I could unfasten the back and pull the bra down into my lap, folding it tightly in one hand to deposit it into my purse, unnoticed. I was very practiced at this move.

"Please don't take off your bra," my date whispered, when I told him my plan. Still a hippie at heart, I once burned my bra, but that night I went to the bathroom to disrobe like a lady.

In the spring, Bob graduated from college with a bachelor's degree in science in urban life. During those eighteen months away from him, the tables turned and he was ready to marry. He sent me flowers, which often were dead by the time I got home. My roommates enjoyed them when they were home. This note was enclosed with the flowers:

> My darling, Judy. Thinking of you flying all around the world.
> I love you. Please come home for my graduation in May.
>
> Love, Bob

I smelled the dead flowers.

He asked his mother to call me. Though she would prefer he find a nice Jewish girl, she knew he loved me and only wanted his happiness.

"Judy, it's Betty. Bob loves you. He wants to marry you."

I had just returned from Paris and already had a trip to Greece planned. "I'm not sure. It sounds dull."

"Just think, you'll buy a house and furniture and be together," she said.

The house and furniture sounded like a prison sentence.

No thanks.

"I'm on my way to Greece. I have to go."

On the arm of a handsome Greek man, I strolled the streets of the Plaka, a picturesque neighborhood in the shadow of the Acropolis in Athens. Syntagma Square bustled with people that day. The sun sparkled, and laughter filled the air. The sweet smell of flowers wafted all around me as each vendor presented me with a daffodil, an orchid, a poppy, a lily, a crocus, and a hyacinth. "For you," each said.

When I got to the end of the street, I had a bouquet.

"You see. They give you flowers because you are so beautiful," my Greek companion said.

It was wonderful to be young.

The countries I visited were exciting, and there were men in every port, but no one measured up to Bob.

We eloped on a hot Labor-Day weekend in 1973. I came in from a trip to find that the air conditioner in my apartment was not working. I called Bob.

"I miss you. I'm coming home. My life is crazy right now. Does your air conditioner work?"

"Yes."

"I'm on the next flight."

Bob picked me up at the airport, and his apartment felt nice and cool.

"We're getting married on Tuesday," he announced the next day.

"Bullshit," I said.

Each day he said, "We're getting married on Tuesday."

Tuesday morning, Bob got up. "We're getting married today. I'm jumping in the shower."

This is insane. I laughed.

Bob called his mother and told her the news.

"Judy and I want to get married. Should we have a Jewish wedding?"

"I don't know, son."

"Judy doesn't know how," he said.

"Well, probably not a good idea then."

"Her parents don't have any money anyway. We're just going to get married."

"Okay, son."

"Let's go." He turned to me.

"What?" With sleepy eyes, I looked at him.

"Get up," he said.

"Jesus, this is crazy." I got up.

Excited by this spur of the moment decision, I showered and put on the only dress I brought with me; a red-flowered silk mini-dress with sheer sleeves. I wore tri-colored platform shoes, blue, green, and cordovan—very leggy, very young, and very gorgeous.

We went downtown to get a marriage license. While waiting for our blood test results, we had lunch in the Hyatt Regency's Polaris restaurant high above Atlanta. We enjoyed the luxurious meal and marveled that we were on this path—not knowing what tomorrow would bring. Bob was steering the way, like he did when we lived together, and I let him. It felt good to have a partner in life again.

With our blood-test results in hand, we crossed the street and entered the office of the justice of the peace who was watching a soap opera blaring on TV.

"We want to get married," Bob said.

The judge looked at our documents.

He called his secretary from the next room. "Bessie, would you come in here, please?"

Bob stood next to me wearing a lovely herringbone jacket, a red tie, and tan slacks. His alligator dress shoes shined. He was a natty dresser in his Zachary clothes.

He glanced down at his belt and shoes as if he'd forgotten something. "Excuse me," he said, and left.

I stood, nervous, fidgeting at the prospect of being left at the altar. Since no one turned down the TV, the loud soap opera filled the void. Both the judge and his secretary watched with renewed interest. I thought Bob had backed out when he reappeared.

"Okay, I'm ready."

Maybe he went to the bathroom or threw up. He could have said a prayer for what he was about to do. I don't know, but with the soap opera blaring, we were wed that day, Tuesday, September 4, 1973, in downtown Atlanta.

Back at the Buford Highway apartment, Bob carried me over the threshold. I held onto the pink champagne we'd picked up at the liquor store down the street. We opened it and toasted our marriage.

"Let's go to Hawaii," he said.

"Okay! I'll call the crew desk."

Bob grinned at me.

I picked up the phone. "Hi, John, it's Judy Coker. I just got married, and I need two weeks off for a honeymoon. And could you arrange a pass for my husband Bob B- E- N- O- W- I- T- Z at the airport in Atlanta? We'll come to D.C. tonight."

Bob called his brother, who also was his boss at that time. "Hey, Jerry, Judy and I just got married. We're taking a honeymoon for two weeks, so I won't be at work. See you, man. Thanks."

After graduation, Bob had gone to work for Jerry in his new business, a chain of childcare centers, so it was easy to get the time off. I don't think I called my mother until after our honeymoon.

We packed our bags and headed to the airport. We flew standby on a full airplane, so we couldn't sit together. We waved to each other across the aisle as we landed in Washington, D.C.

I unlocked the door to my apartment in Alexandria, Virginia. "Bob and I just got married!"

"Well, you can't stay here on your wedding night," my roommate Julie hollered. "How unromantic."

"She's right." I nodded.

"Call the Shoreham downtown," Julie said. "I spent Mardi Gras there. It's great,"

At midnight we checked into the Shoreham honeymoon suite. Champagne, flowers, and chocolates greeted us.

"I need a diamond ring," I told Bob the next day.

"Okay. I'll call Uncle Sol. We'll go see him in Chicago on our way to Hawaii."

Uncle Sol owned a jewelry store on Wabash Avenue in Chicago. Bob had given me a Yemenite gold band he'd bought in Israel when he visited there a year ago. It became my wedding band, but I wanted a diamond. We spent one night in Chicago, met with Uncle Sol, ordered the ring, then flew to Las Vegas for a couple of nights.

Dolled up and gorgeous, we walked into the Flamingo Casino our first night in Vegas.

"May I take your picture?" the photographer said.

"No. It costs too much," Bob whispered.

"But it's our honeymoon," I said.

"Your honeymoon," she said. "You need a picture,"

"No, thanks," Bob said.

It was seventeen dollars.

"Someday you'll want this picture," the photographer said.

She was right.

We flew to Los Angeles, Honolulu, and Hilo, using my airline discount to stay in all the beautiful honeymoon suites. At twenty-four, we were barely old enough to rent a small car to drive around the island of Oahu.

We took a road that followed the shoreline of the island. It took us to the "unpaved road." On the map it looked like a short distance. Although the sign warned us, "Do Not Enter," we drove on. We met a motorcyclist who said, "It's a little narrow up ahead."

When we approached the narrow passage, the sea sprayed me as I opened the door to get out and guide Bob forward. I slid to the front with my backside against the car as my flip flops skated on the sandy edge of the road. The wheels barely fit on the path, as the dark blue Pacific Ocean crashed waves onto the rocks below us. I motioned for Bob to turn the wheels out to sea to get past a boulder. He studied me for a few minutes, questioning his trust of me. *Was I sending him plunging below?*

"Come on." I laughed.

Hesitant at first, he turned the wheel, first to the right, out to sea. As soon as the front wheel passed the rock, I pointed him away from the edge. The back wheel clipped the side of the boulder, but he cleared it.

When I got back into the car, we congratulated each other on our teamwork. The only other choice was to drive in reverse for miles. He followed my direction to get past the obstacle. That was the first of many obstacles to come.

Bob on Waikiki beach

It was a wonderful adventure. Each day was new and fresh and unplanned. The only pictures of our wedding and honeymoon are four snapshots from my Kodak Brownie Starmite Camera I got when I was in high school.

I posed on Waikiki Beach in front of the Royal Hawaiian Hotel, the iconic pink palace, wearing my pink thong bikini that I had bought in Rio de Janeiro. On the Big Island, Bob and I walked on the lava scorched Desolation Trail of Kilauea, the volcano in Hilo, and another tourist snapped our picture.

There were no great photographs of such a momentous event, but the third one—of us in front of Oahu's Polynesian Cultural Center outside Honolulu—stands on our bookcase today. Our young faces smile, full of hope and adventure. I'm wearing hot pants, a babushka, and no bra under that halter top. The snapshot, now faded by the years, shows our slender bodies holding fast to each other, framed by the little grass shack.

When we got back to D.C., I faced the task of moving, but it just didn't make sense. I kept my apartment in Virginia and commuted to Atlanta to see my new husband on my days off. Bob had asked me to convert to Judaism, so I started classes at The Washington National Hebrew Congregation on Massachusetts Avenue in Washington, D.C. It was a huge congregation with five rabbis. I went to the model Seder (a feast that marks the beginning of Passover), bought my prayer books, and attended services on Friday nights. It was time to graduate after six weeks, but I had missed three classes because I was flying.

1973, Bob and I on our honeymoon

"Live Jewishly," Rabbi Fink told me.

Bob was very spiritual. So were his parents, his brother Jerry, Jerry's wife Sandra, and his kid brother David. Though this was a new step for me, it was a logical religion, not steeped in faith, but in history, and many religions borrowed from it.

I thought of the rabbi's advice while driving into the Baltimore airport. I remembered the shock on hearing the news that six Israeli athletes had been murdered at the Munich Olympic Games in 1972. Mark Spitz, the Jewish-American swimmer, was escorted to safety. The film I saw that night was horrifying. They were just kids. How deep could the hatred be? I was joining that minority.

What was I signing up for?

Los Angeles
1973-1974

Bob's business in childcare expanded to the Los Angeles area. After we'd been married for six months, we moved to Newport Beach, California, and I transferred from Washington, D.C., to Los Angeles for my domicile with United Air Lines. We celebrated our first wedding anniversary in Newport Beach. By now Bob spent much of his time traveling for Mini-Skools, his brother's company. I was flying out of L.A. We were both on the road.

Los Angeles in the '70s was another exciting place to be. The summer months on the beaches of Southern California were gray, with the sun breaking through the fog at noon—"June Gloom." The desert landscape had no trees, only scrub brush. It took some getting used to. We had taken a second honeymoon to Portugal and Casablanca while we lived on the east coast, but once we moved to L.A., all our travels were out West.

We rafted down the Colorado River through the Grand Canyon, went deep sea fishing in Hawaii, and skied the Colorado Rockies. We drove the coastline up to San Francisco and took road trips to Mexico. We fell in love with the West.

In the meantime, the Watergate scandal grew every day as it was reported by Washington Post journalists Bob Woodward and Carl Bernstein. President Nixon, rather than face impeachment, resigned from office on August 9, 1974, as the only President in U.S. history to do so.

Bob and I were newlyweds living in Newport Beach, just up the coast from San Clemente, the Western White House. We drove to Marine Corps Air Station El Toro to see Nixon come home to California in disgrace. The grandstands were full of people there to welcome him home as he stepped off Air Force One and made his salute to the crowd—arms outstretched and fingers in a peace sign. Staunch supporters Bob and I were not, but it was an opportunity to see history unfold just down the street from where we lived.

Looking back at my lifestyle, flying all over the world, I spent little time with my husband because he travelled, too. We were both very independent.

Bob's family accepted me after a year of trying to discourage him from pursuing this relationship, hoping he would see that this *goyishe shiksa* girlfriend was not for him.

I was the first to break the family's ethnicity, a real pioneer. Bob's father Hal asked us to meet him in their home in Orlando for marriage counseling. He was a social worker after all. Losing patience with this crowd, I was way ahead of him on all the points he wanted to cover. I think he found my spit fire manner endearing.

"You need to apply for a credit card," Hal said.

"I have one," I said. In fact, we had used my credit card, along with my airline discounts, for our honeymoon.

"You should look at some of the local temples and choose one you like."

"We'll find one, eventually."

He laughed. "Well, if you have any questions, ask Judy," was his advice to Bob.

Hal and Betty moved to California the year after Bob and I did. Jerry and Sandra moved there a few months later. We went to the temple with the family for High Holy Days and Passover. I learned a few prayers and songs that I could recite with the congregation. The family got together almost every weekend, and I started to feel smothered.

"You're a hypocrite," was my mother's take on the situation. "Even though your name means Jewess, you'll never be a Jew."

Okay, great, now we got that settled.

The Mountain Creek Baptist Church is where my family went to services. All the church suppers and breakfasts were held at the log cabin social hall where the preacher lived upstairs for a time before they built the parish.

Mother hosted a bridal shower for

Bob and I at my parents' house before the bridal shower, 1973

me at the log cabin, a few months after Bob and I were married. Except for my cousin Ann, I had not seen some of my high school friends for years. They showed up full of questions about the Jewish boy I had married. It was awkward. They all wanted to know about my life as a flight attendant. I felt like a freak, then Bob walked in with Mother at the end of the night.

She introduced him to everyone. I stood frozen, staring at him as if he were a stranger. Mother was showing him all the gifts, and he pretended interest, but kept glancing over to me, wondering why I didn't come up to him. He looked at me and gestured with his arms wide in a question.

What the hell have I done? Did I really marry that guy? Are those our dishes?

Damn.

Coffee, Tea, or Me
A Day in the Life of a Flight Attendant

I worked for United Airlines for more than ten years. I flew out of D.C. two years, then I transferred to Los Angeles after Bob and I married. I flew a few puddle jumpers on both coasts of the mainland. These narrow-body aircraft were the 737s and 727s. Then I became overwater qualified and flew LAX-HNL (Honolulu) exclusively on 747s and DC-10s for my last eight years of employment.

The book *Coffee, Tea or Me*, published in the late 1960s, was a fictional account of the adventures of young, beautiful airline stewardesses, minus any politically correct restraints. In fact, the title comes from an old airline joke: A stewardess enters the cockpit of a commercial airplane and asks the pilot, "Coffee, tea or me?" The pilot says, "Whichever is easier to make."

The author later wrote about his surprise that his imaginative narrative would "…cause anxious mothers to forbid their daughters from becoming stewardesses, spawn airline protest groups, have its title inducted into the public vocabulary…."

Airline travel was glamorous and fun most of the time, but there also were a few alarming episodes during my decade in the sky. As good fortune would have it, I was never involved in a crash. The celebrities on board were some of my favorite memories of that time.

***

Laughing, drinking, and having fun, Michael Douglas sat in first class with Brenda Vacarro on his lap for most of a flight from L.A. to San Francisco. He was filming the TV show "The Streets of San Francisco" at that time.

***

"Leading man" of the '60s beach movies Troy Donahue commuted from Monterey, California, to L.A. He was a heartthrob. Tall, blond, and tanned, his blue eyes sparkled as he ducked so as not to hit his head when he boarded. Sitting without speaking, he just wanted to get home.

1976, wearing United Airlines domestic uniform designed by Stan Herman

***

In 1972 on a flight from New York to Los Angeles, John Travolta, with his black curls and high energy, ran down the aisles with the whole cast of the Broadway musical *Grease*. They took over the airplane, laughing and singing. It looked like an episode of the TV show "Glee." Everyone loved them.

***

Pistol Pete Maravich of the Atlanta Hawks was on my flight headed to his next game with teammate Jim Washington. The Pistol was the most exciting player in the National Basketball Association in 1972. He averaged 43 points per game when he played for Louisiana State University as a freshman in 1966, before he entered the NBA.

He was seated in coach when I offered him a Coke from the beverage cart. Right away I recognized him and wanted to talk basketball. "I averaged twenty-seven points a game and made all-state in high school," I said, grinning inside at my exaggeration.

After I placed his drink on his tray table, he took my hand, pressed it to his lips, and planted a wet, sloppy kiss. "Do you still play today?"

"No."

"Well, I do," he said, with a smile.

***

By the time we flew into L.A., the sun had already set. I was "deadheading" home off a trip, meaning my work schedule ended in another city, but I needed to get back to my home base for the next day's trip. The airlines would fly nonworking crewmembers in the first-class cabin to get them in position for their next flight.

Shots rang out above my head in seat 4A. I screamed and threw my book across the aisle. "Ahhhh! What the fuck?"

Everyone looked around, but we could not discover where the shots came from. Was it real? Did we imagine it? Everyone had the same look on their faces, and we sat there like sheep through the rest of the flight.

When I got off the airplane, I looked back. Two pilots were examining the fuselage in first class. Above one window were about fifty blackened holes and chipped paint. That was right above seat 4A where I was sitting. It was a lightning strike, the captain told me when he came in to the terminal.

On another flight coming in for landing in Fresno, California, a tire blew-out and we skidded and swerved, tires screeching, as people screamed and held onto anything they could reach. There were no injuries except bumps and bruises, but as they say in the industry, "Any landing you can walk away from is a good one."

***

Hijacking was common in the '70s, and flight attendants were taught to comply, comply, comply to survive. Very different from what flight attendants are taught today. They are trained to thwart the assailant.

Hijackers in the '70s wanted to go to Cuba. There were eighty-two Cuban hijackings in the '60s and '70s. Soon pilots began landing in Florida and telling the hijacker he was in Cuba, and he was led off in handcuffs.

The most famous hijacker was D. B. Cooper. In 1971 he extorted $200,000 from Northwest Orient Airlines. He demanded that the pilot drop below 20,000 feet so the rear door below the fuselage of the 727 could be opened. He went down the stairs with twenty-one pounds of twenty-dollar bills strapped to his back. He jumped and was never seen again.

There was no security in those days. Anyone could walk on board with a bomb. If anyone said the word, "bomb," the flight attendants were to notify the authorities, and the offender would be led off the airplane by police. We were the security.

***

As I stood in the aisle directing the boarding coach passengers, a drunk, portly man passed by me and took his seat on the aisle. At the same moment he sat down, his hands went up my dress all the way to my breasts, and he fondled every inch of me. I screamed, and he pretended it wasn't him. An agent in charge of boarding came to my defense and led the apologetic man off the airplane.

"I'm sorry," he said. "I'm sorry."

The boarding agents and the flight attendants handled most problems that might arise with the public.

***

On a thirty-six-hour layover in Tampa, Florida, I joined the crew for an afternoon at Busch Gardens. Since the layover was more than twenty-four hours, we were legal to drink. It was lunchtime, and we were having fun drinking and laughing when I made the mistake of climbing on a table to dance.

"Please get down. You need to leave," the manager said.

"Yeah, well, I've been thrown out of nicer places than this. Yeah, we're going," I said, as we wobbled out.

***

With a $200 loan from the credit union and my airline discount, I vacationed in Mexico. On the beach in Acapulco, five Mexicans held my parachute until it filled with air, then let it go, and I ascended as the boat increased speed out to the bay. It was my first time parasailing, and I had drunk too many piña coladas. My harness was not well-cinched so one leg stood out sideways and fell asleep. The only way to get down was to pull a release rope hanging above my left shoulder to deflate the chute enough to descend.

After 45 minutes, I was ready to come down. They flew me over the beach, and I tried to land by pulling with all my strength on that rope. The five Mexican men jumped to grab my feet and pull me down. I could not hold onto the rope and flew back up for another turn. Now I was afraid.

On the next pass over the beach, the boat somehow managed to bring me in lower. I pulled the rope with all my might, and the boys grabbed me and brought me in. Once I was on the ground, ten male hands were all over my bikini-clad body trying to uncinch my chute or my bikini, whichever came first.

***

Honolulu, Hawaii, was my home away from home for eight years. I flew in every week. Photos of Frank Sinatra were displayed throughout the dining room of Luigi's Italian Restaurant.

It was rumored that the mafia owned Luigi's and ran drugs out of there. You could order cocaine with dinner.

Cindy Lew and I tested that rumor one night and ordered coke with our fried mozzarella. It came on a plate under a napkin. Cindy took the coke, put twenty dollars under the napkin, and the waiter picked it up. She opened the small pack and thought it was not enough and mouthed off to the maître d'.

Immediately four guys surrounded us and asked us to leave. Cindy, always ready for a fight, resisted. One man pulled her bandeau top down exposing her breasts to humiliate her. "Get your goddamned hands off me, motherfuckers. I want my money back," Cindy screamed.

Then they threw us out.

We never went back there. I thought we might be murdered.

The Stop Light was a Honolulu strip club where Cindy and I got into another fight. This time the manager threw the guy out.

A tiny Asian dancer provided the floor show at The Stop Light. She could shoot an egg across the stage with her vagina. A guy on the other side would catch it. That was her act. Another larger Caucasian dancer in pasties would swing her breasts in opposite directions. Still another dancer would shoot breast milk out into the audience. The guys loved it.

"Get your hands off me! Get the fuck off me. Stop touching me," Cindy shouted. The guy sitting behind us was fondling Cindy, who was scantily clad, as was I.

"Okay, out of here." The manager put a stop to it.

We both wore shorts and halter tops with no bra. Maybe he thought we were part of the show. There were few women in the audience. We went just to see something different from The Don Ho show. It was different, all right.

The next day as we were leaving on the crew bus for the airport, we spotted one of the strippers in her car with her little daughter in the back seat. She went into the bank, maybe to deposit her cash from the night before. She looked very ordinary in clothes.

***

Clint Eastwood made a big entrance on the 747 to Honolulu one morning.

"Hello, love, how are you?" he said.

"Great, now that you're here." I gave him a beaming smile. "May I take your bags?"

Clint was tall and brawny with arms flexed holding two bags "They're heavy. Show me where to put them."

I led him to the first-class closet.

For the entire flight, he sat with his nose in a book while I paced the cabin waiting for him to get up so I could talk to him. After six hours, the pilot made his final approach announcement, and Clint went into the bathroom. I waited outside the door and ambushed him when he came out.

"Mr. Eastwood, would you mind posing for a picture?"

"Sure."

"Let's go upstairs to the lounge. John, come on, bring your camera." I said to another flight attendant.

Clint followed me up the spiral stairs to the lounge. I posed with my arms wrapped around his waist as I stood beside him. He hugged me, too.

1974, Clint Eastwood and I onboard 747 to Honolulu

"Ah, remember the wonderful weekend in Hawaii," he said.

"I wish." I gazed up at him.

He grinned. The picture snapped. When I saw the picture later, Clint had his red carpet smile, and I looked like I would take a bite out of him. I probably would have, given half a chance.

We hurried back downstairs for landing. At the end of the flight, I tried to return his bags to him from the closet, but he had heavy weights in each one. He picked them up with ease.

Clint was a rock. Now I know why.

***

Beau Bridges sat with his wife in first class. He stopped me as I walked past.

"Isn't there a kitchen on-board the 747?"

"Yes, there is. It's below deck. We take the elevator down."

"I would love to see it."

"Come on. I'll give you a tour."

"Let's go see," Beau said to his wife.

"I do not want to see the kitchen," she said, yawning.

"Come on. It'll be fun." He stood up.

"No." She returned to her book.

"Come on, Mr. Bridges, I'll take you." I led him to the elevator.

We stood cheek to cheek in the tiny elevator designed for one person.

"This is cool," he said.

"Yes, it is." I felt his breath on my neck.

When we reached the first-class kitchen, I opened the elevator door. Ann, the galley-girl, was there loading racks into the ovens. "We can't have this many people down here. I'll be back," she said.

She got on the elevator and ascended, leaving Beau and me to tour and talk.

"Look at all the ovens. This is where you cook the food?" Beau strode past the line of ovens, counting them.

"That's right, and we put the racks into the carts and send them up the elevator."

Beau was having so much fun, I almost gave him some oven mitts to put on. He was very interested in the galley operation and where all the doors led.

"Behind this wall of cabinets is cargo. Up here you can actually open the ceiling panels and access the cockpit," I said.

"Wow. Unbelievable."

"Those walls fold and collapse and can be reconfigured." I pointed.

"So I could get to the cockpit if I climbed up here and opened that ceiling?" He touched the recessed steps in the wall above the sink.

"Only in an emergency. It's an escape route in case the elevators are damaged. You can also deactivate the elevators and climb up the ladder inside the second shaft. One elevator is for humans, the second is for carts only. The cockpit exit is used in extreme situations like a hijacking or a crash."

"Oh, yeah, I get it."

"Sometimes the pilots will come down here to access the space and check the mechanics of the instrument panel. That access has multi-functions."

"Too cool."

"There's another galley in coach. Want to see? It's much bigger," I said, as Ann returned to finish loading the ovens.

"Yes." Beau followed me through the coach section to the elevators. The coach passengers dropped their jaws to see Beau Bridges saunter down the aisle. In the coach galley, he was equally fascinated.

After a brief tour, we returned to first class, and Beau took his seat next to his wife.

"You should have come. That was interesting," he said.

She looked at me and returned to her book, as Beau took my hand and covered it with his other hand.

"Thank you so much." He looked deep into my eyes.

What a gentleman and a dreamboat.

***

Bob Dylan sat in first class reading the paper.

"Good morning, Mr. Dylan. May I offer you a drink?"

"No thanks. Just water," he said, squinting as if pained.

I brought him a glass of water.

"So, what are you doing in Hawaii? Do you have a concert?"

He squinted again. More like a wince. "No, just touring."

"Oh, touring the islands. Great. Could I have your autograph?"

He wrote on United Airlines stationery, "To

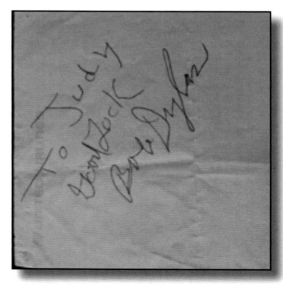

1975, Bob Dylan's autograph on United Airlines Stationery

Judy, Good Luck, Bob Dylan."

In his song "115th Dream," about the discovery of America, Bob Dylan wrote, "I saw three ships a sailin'.... I just said, 'Good luck.' "

The day after Bob Dylan's flight, I read an article in the *Los Angeles Times* about his wife going to Hawaii with their five children and leaving him. I'm sure he was there to bring her home—probably the reason he squinted at my nosy question.

***

On his way to Honolulu, Dickey Betts sat in the 747 upstairs, first-class lounge wearing a cowboy hat, jeans, and an open shirt collar that framed his chain necklace.

"Mr. Wong?" I said.

"Do I look like Mr. Wong?"

"No." I laughed. "I'm just reading the manifest. You look like a musician. What's your name?"

"Dickey Betts."

"May I offer you a drink, Mr. Betts?"

"Sure, I'll have a scotch straight up."

"What band do you play with?"

"The Doobie Brothers."

In the next few days after that flight, I saw on television that Dicky Betts was with the "Allman Brothers Band" instead. This was in 1976, when Gregg Allman left the band and testified in court against his drug dealer and road manager, which the bandmates saw as a betrayal. The court hearings, drug testimony, and other sordid details of the relationships of the band members played out every day on the news in L.A.

Dickey Betts did not want to drop that name on me. He would rather be Mr. Wong.

***

A bodyguard blocked my approach to South Korean Premier Kim Jong-pil in first class.

"He doesn't want anything," the bodyguard said.
"Would he like a drink?" I said.
"No. We'll let you know."

For the entire flight, three guards stood in the aisle like soldiers looking all around guarding the premier, except for takeoff and landing (federal regulations).

***

Folk singer John Denver was enjoying musical success with "Rocky Mountain High" and other songs celebrating his Colorado lifestyle, as well as starring in the movie "Oh, God!" with George Burns. He boarded our flight wearing a red ski vest and posed for pictures with the entire crew. He was very personable.

"What's George Burns like?" I said, curious about the old vaudevillian who started acting in 1902.

"Oh, he's great. What a pro."

"What did you think about your part in that movie?"

"Well, I believed in myself so it was easy to do."

I ran into John another time in Aspen where he lived. With a hand full of magazines at checkout, he turned around, took one look at me, and dropped all of them.

I may have been standing too close.

1978, John Denver onboard 747 to Honolulu

***

Brook Shields was just a little girl travelling with her mom in coach when I encountered her. All the flight crew circled the coach cabin to get a look at the child actress. She was a phenomenon, and her mom watched her like a hawk.

***

Loretta Lynn sat with her husband in first class.

"I love your music," I said as I put out my hand to shake hers.

She didn't want to but smiled, bothered, and extended a cold, bony, lifeless hand.

***

Actress Barbara Eden was tiny with her white powdered face, heavy eye makeup, and red lips. Her snow-white arms seemed to glow all the way to her perfectly manicured fingertips. She walked fast to keep from falling forward by the weight of her large breasts.

Twenty years had passed since she played the lead in the television series *I Dream of Jeannie*, but she was unchanged, a porcelain doll.

***

Big, strong Lyle Alzado was riding in coach. He was on his way to play in the National Football League Pro Bowl in Hawaii.

"You're beautiful. I love your red hair," he said. "How long are you in Hawaii?"

"I'll be here overnight. I think you know my husband," I said. "He visited you in Denver when you worked together on the Special Olympics. His business was one of the sponsors, and you were the spokesperson."

"Oh, yeah." His face dropped as he recalled.

"I'll tell him you said hello."

"Yeah, do that."

We didn't speak again on the flight, and he waved goodbye and smiled as he deplaned.

***

Sometimes the thick tule fog, named for the tule grass of the Central Valley, would roll into Los Angeles after a heavy rain, and we would divert to Las Vegas for the night. The fog was a leading cause of weather-related accidents in California. I always had a glittery dress in my bag for those occasions in Las Vegas. We saw Shirley McClaine, Bill Cosby, Wayne Newton, and Elvis.

Flight attendants got in free because we decorated the bar, but we had to give the guy working the door a tip or he would seat us behind a post.

***

In 1974, a "streaker" ran across the stage of the Academy Awards ceremony behind David Niven as he was introducing Elizabeth Taylor. "Isn't it fascinating that the only laugh that young man will get is by stripping off and showing his shortcomings," Niven quipped.

Professional baseball fields and basketball courts had their share of the naked, too. One of the Honolulu flight attendants streaked down the 747 aisle from the first-class bathroom to the coach bathroom, where someone had placed her clothes. She came out fully dressed and pretended it wasn't her. She was fired anyway.

***

We were on our way home from Honolulu when the pilot, with a flashlight in his hand, came out of the cockpit into the upstairs first-class lounge of the 747. He opened a ceiling panel and looked around. A light on top of the fuselage had broken off during the flight. We were past the point of no return so he plugged the hole with a dinner tray. It stayed suctioned to the ceiling all the way home.

Amazed by the pilot's ingenuity, I kept my eye on the tray each time I came up to the lounge.

***

Hula's Bar & Lei Stand in Honolulu was a popular gay bar under a banyan tree with twinkle lights and mirrors. Cindy and I went to hear disco music and dance to the psychedelic lights. The music was thumping. The gay bars always had the best music.

"Would you like to dance?" A girl with short hair smiled at me.

"No, thanks," I said.

This was my first lesbian encounter, and I wasn't sure how to behave. I stood watching the crowd, which was mixed with gays and straights. I danced in a group with Cindy and some guys when the girl with the short hair came back with a drink in her hand.

"Would you like a drink?" she said.

"Sure." I couldn't be rude to her. She just wanted to dance, and she would not take no for an answer.

"Okay, let's go," I said.

I gave in and danced with her. She was nice enough and bought me drinks, but it was weird. I was glad to leave.

***

Halloween in Hawaii was an event with costumes and all-night parties. Every bar had a contest, and they were well attended. The winner of one of the contests was a three-legged man. He cracked up everyone.

David Kopay, famous running back in the NFL, who in 1975 became one of the first professional athletes to come out as gay, sang "The Big Bamboo" with a band in one of the bars we went to. The song was a joke, and he was a pretty good singer. He was married for a short time to one of the female supervisors of flight attendants in Washington, D.C. We saw the popular "Unknown Comic" one night. He wore a paper bag with eyeholes over his head, a funny routine. He appeared on The Gong Show presented by Chuck Barris.

The comedian inspired a calendar that our flight crew published one year. It featured all the girls dressed in either bathing suits or lingerie, and we wore paper bags over our heads. One Black steward wearing flame embellished underwear lay across the floor.

The calendar was famous that year.

Me (in striped suit) posing with coworkers for United Airlines Calendar, 1976

1976, calendar pose without our bags

***

On my way to the Liberty House, a department store on Kalakaua Avenue in Honolulu, a guy scooped me up in his arms, holding me high in the air.

"You're beautiful," he said.

"Unhand me, you fiend." I struggled to get free.

I wore beach attire—a halter top with matching panties and a long, hip-hugger skirt with a slit all the way to the waist. I must have been a show-stopper on that crowded street.

***

Captain Lou Shapiro was retiring at age 60, mandatory for pilots. He hosted a week-long party in the penthouse of the Marine Surf Waikiki Hotel, the crew's home in Honolulu. He arranged for belly dancers, food, and liquor every night for all the crews who came through.

"I can't believe it's over," he said. "I feel like a 20-year-old trapped in a 60-year-old body."

The Friendly Skies

In 1973 when Bob and I moved to Newport Beach, California, he traveled every week in his new job as operations manager in his family's childcare business, and I flew out of Los Angeles to Honolulu. Sometimes we didn't see each other for weeks. I was lonely in my new dwelling, often flying all day to come home to an empty apartment.

I wasn't there for long though. My schedule included Hilo, Hawaii, turnarounds, which meant 16 hours on duty. That stretched to an 18-hour day with travel back and forth to the airport. The Hilo-turnaround was held by the most senior flight attendants because they could work only seven days a month to earn the 75-hour minimum flight time.

We bid on a flight schedule each month and were assigned by seniority.

Most of the time, I bid two-day trips back-to-back so I had three days off a week. I was still on reserve every other month, which meant the crew desk assigned my trips. If I got the Hilo-turn after a four-day schedule, it was a killer.

I remember getting that call from the crew desk to fly to Hilo. I cried as I sat in the bathtub getting ready for the long day. Only when Bob came in to make love to me in the tub did I cheer up and drive off to face that trip.

Another time I woke up to find the bedside phone hanging down on the floor. I was supposed to work that day, and something told me I had missed a trip, which guaranteed that the supervisor would place a warning letter in my file.

I called the crew desk. "Do you have a flight for me today?"

"Yeah, I tried to call you at 3:00 a.m. for an 8:00 a.m. departure. We could tell you were talking in your sleep."

"I don't remember, but my phone was off the hook when I woke up. Do you have something for me now?"

"No. We're covered. Relax. We'll call you tomorrow."

Flying everyday through different time zones could be very tiring. Sometimes I didn't know if I was coming or going until I looked at the sign on the 405 Freeway. If it said South, I was going home.

For the first six years of our marriage, I wanted to start a family and Bob put us on a "two-year-plan."

"Let's wait two years," he said.

After three of those "two-year-plans," I came up with my own plan and stopped taking birth control pills, drinking alcohol, and smoking. I wanted a baby.

On March 2, 1981, Bob and I checked into a beautiful, ocean-view birthing-room at Hoag Hospital, high atop the cliffs overlooking Newport Beach. The baby's head lodged against my lower spine—back labor.

"Rub my back hard, Bob."

"I feel the baby's head in your back. I'm afraid to push too hard."

"Just push anyway."

Bob rubbed my back for six hours until his back ached from bending over me. Then Shayne was born.

As a new mom, I enjoyed staying home. Shayne slept through the night, sat in her stroller, and hardly fussed about anything. During my maternity leave, I met other new moms at play groups in the park. I loved having a job and not working, but after eighteen months my United Airlines leave expired. I needed to hire a nanny. I must have talked to one hundred people.

"Are you going to interview the entire population of Santa Ana?" Bob said.

"I can't find anybody I can trust."

"There must be someone."

"No. Either they don't speak English or they're too old. I'm not sure I can do this. I don't want to leave Shayne. You're traveling. I'm traveling. Somebody needs to stay home with the baby."

"Up to you," Bob said.

I met with my supervisor to discuss my options. "Can I extend my leave again?" I said.

"No. We need all our staff for the season, but if you come back to work for a few months, maybe you can take a personal leave, or maybe we can buy out your contract," he said.

"A few months?"

"Yes, and you would have to go back to Chicago for two weeks to retrain."

In 1978, the Airline Deregulation Act changed the industry. Government subsidies were gone, and so were the empty seats. Airlines had to compete and cut labor costs. Some went out of business, others merged, and flights became crowded. United offered flight attendants lump sum payments to quit, so they could pay "B-scale" workers less to do the same job. Torn to the quick, I loved my job, but I loved my baby more.

"I'm thinking… of quitting, but I'm afraid to… make that decision."

My supervisor raised his eyebrows. "I'll give you two weeks to decide. Talk to the psychologist at the health center. Maybe he can help you."

Later that week I drove into the crew parking lot, up to a gray, stark building with no windows. I slunk into the psychologist's stuffy office and sat across from him. He smiled and listened as I explained my problem.

"I don't think I can leave my baby at home with a stranger, but I'm afraid to quit my job," I told him. "I've been here ten years. I fly to Hawaii every week. I have seniority, free travel, insurance, and retirement. How can I walk away?"

"Answer two questions," he said.

"Do you have to work?"

"Well, no."

"Is your marriage secure?"

"Yes, I think so."

"Well, then your answer should be obvious."

I quit my job, but it was a huge loss. No more free passes and extra income.

God, what was I doing, making myself completely dependent on Bob for everything?

The psychologist should have asked the third question: "Did you know that you can make thirty-thousand dollars cash by selling your contract and have free passes for the rest of your life if you just go back to work for two months?"

That's exactly what many flight attendants in my position did. Still I was much happier after I made my decision.

I went on to spend the '80s with my legs in the air either making babies or having babies. We had three children in seven years.

My Son the Actor

"We are on our final approach to Boston," the flight attendant announces.

My husband, Bob, is shuffling his newspaper beside me. In the middle seat of an over-booked flight, angling for elbow room on the armrest, with my knees pushed into the seat in front me, I remember a different time in air travel.

Boston breaks through the clouds. A fine city, but we will not be touring today. Instead, we're driving sixty miles north to Manchester, New Hampshire.

Our son, Brett, is on stage there in *Million Dollar Quartet* at the Palace Theater. Bob and I will see four shows—one Friday night, two Saturday, and a Father's Day matinee.

Brett started acting when he was eight, in "Snow White and the Seven Dwarfs," in which he cried in character when Snow White died.

"Mom, I cried real tears," he said.

That same year he played a surfer dude in a children's production at Cartersville's Grand Theater. He wore Levi's with a Hawaiian shirt.

"Yeah, surf's up," he said with a little hip thrust, as if he were on a board.

Brett was born in Newport Beach, California, where Bob and I had moved as newlyweds. I was a flight attendant based in Los Angeles.

Like most young women who moved to L.A., I wanted to be a movie star. I did some modeling when the apartment complex where we lived made a new brochure. I was wrapped in a towel in the sauna for one shot, wearing a leotard and riding a stationary bike in the second photo, and dressed for tennis with the pro for the back cover

Nina Blanchard, the famous modeling agent in Los Angeles, thumbed through my portfolio and read my résumé. "You're a flight attendant? Where do you fly?"

"Honolulu," I said.

"Why do you want to do this? You already have a great job." She took off her glasses and ran her fingers through her bleached blonde curls.

"I need to do more. On the airplane, I watch life go by. People get off the airplane and go somewhere. I turn around and fly home."

She studied me for a second, then pushed my portfolio back to me. "These are pictures of an actress. You need to take acting lessons. You can do it all your life." She wished me luck, and added: "You'll meet people from the industry on your flights. Introduce yourself. You're already too old to model."

I was twenty-eight.

I enrolled in the University of California, Irvine, to pursue a degree in drama. I flew all-nighters to make a nine a.m. class. Ten years older than most students, I was closer to the age of my professors.

Along with many stage performances at UCI, I played a nurse in a student film at the University of Southern California: "Boy with Wings," filmed at Cedars-Sinai Medical Center. I appeared in "Sweet Charity" at the Westminster Playhouse with two retired Las Vegas show girls from *Les Folies Bergere*, who danced on stage in pasties and heavy headdresses for years before retiring to the stages of Los Angeles. They taught me a lot about dance and instructed me to just "sell it."

I almost sold it on one audition.

As I approached a small bungalow in Hollywood for the audition, a pretty blonde raced past me.

"Don't go in there," she said.

Was she talking to me?

A handsome man answered the door of the bungalow, and we exchanged pleasantries in the living room. "You'll play a woman who's getting older and losing her looks. She's depressed, looking at herself in the mirror," he said. "Come in the bathroom. Let me see what you can do."

The director stood next to me, as I frowned into the mirror and brushed my hair forward. I squinted and pulled back my face with my hands, turning side to side. I gave a little sigh and shot a bird at the mirror.

"Good. Come back into the living room. We need to talk about a few other things."

He sat down next to me on the couch and told me the film had nudity. When I didn't object, he asked me to take off my blouse. I did.

"Would you mind taking off your bra? I need to see your breasts."

I took off my bra and sat there topless. He smiled like a fiend. I looked at his lap, saw his erection, and panicked.

I jumped up, grabbing my shirt for cover. As I ran out the door, still buttoning my shirt while holding my bra, I saw a young girl coming up the walk to the house.

"Don't go in there," I warned.

The industry has a seedy side. When Brett in college started auditioning for independent filmmakers in Atlanta, I advised him not to go on auditions in private houses alone.

The pinnacle of my acting career was when I was an extra getting union wages on the TV show "Archie Bunker's Place," starring Carroll O'Connor at CBS Studios.

"Mr. O'Connor, I have always admired your work," I said when I saw an opening.

He shook my hand and walked away.

"What are you doing?" the director said, running over. "You don't talk to the star. You are supposed to be a professional. If everyone ogled the star, we wouldn't get anything done."

The director later apologized, but CBS never called me back. I had an eighteen-month-old baby, Shayne, at home, and my babysitter made more money than I did that day.

I had three children in seven years, and I retired from flying and acting to stay home as a full-time mom. We moved across the country when Bob took a job in Cartersville, Georgia.

The town has a vibrant community theater with the Pumphouse Players and the Grand Theater. I started acting again.

My director needed a boy to play a twelve-year-old in "Lost in Yonkers." My influence on Brett's career began. "My nine-year-old son can do it."

Brett, my youngest, born when I was thirty-nine, played my grandson.

He took piano lessons, as did his two older sisters, Shayne and Kristy, and they all performed at the local theater. As a high school senior, Brett was leading man, Tony, in *West Side Story*, and Bob appeared alongside him as Lieutenant Shrank.

My daughters gave up the stage, but Brett took his University of Georgia drama degree to New York to make it a career.

He learned to play guitar as a teenager when he wanted a break from the piano. I bought him his first electric Squier by Fender, and he signed up for lessons with a musician who sometimes forgot to show up. As Brett became more proficient, he sold the beginner Squier and purchased a Fender Stratocaster in deep purple.

He later added acoustic and bass guitars to his collection, and he is the lead singer in a new band.

Brett recently toured the country as the lead vocalist in "Rockin' Road to Dublin," an original extravaganza, complete with Irish river dancers that we hope makes it to Broadway. Bob and I saw that show in Sacramento for Brett's birthday, then in Austin, Macon, Montgomery and Fort Lauderdale.

In June, Brett had a four-week engagement of *Million Dollar Quartet* in New Hampshire. He called me when he got the part.

"Mom, Carl Perkins was a guitar virtuoso. He played lead guitar for all his music. I had to learn about twenty-three songs, not to mention all the dialogue," he said. Brett agreed to cut his hair for the part and got to play the guitar solos for Elvis and Johnny Cash as well as his character, Perkins.

Unless you are a musician or a music lover, you might not remember Carl Perkins, who wrote "Blue Suede Shoes" but never enjoyed the fame Elvis did for that song.

People think Elvis wrote it. The drama plays out on stage in *Million Dollar Quartet*—Perkins, Elvis, Cash, and Jerry Lee Lewis—with Brett as Perkins playing "Blue Suede Shoes" on a Les Paul electric guitar.

While in Manchester, we listened to a rough cut of Brett's new album, played through our rental car's speakers from a file on his phone. "You know the songs, but I have changed some of the arrangements, adding harmony and a piano," he said.

While I listened to the familiar tunes, I was reminded of the stages where he played them—Nashville, Austin, New Orleans, and Cartersville.

Brett wrote "Something to Believe In," and tears filled my eyes as it played.

"Brett, that is beautiful. I am so proud of you."

"Mom, are you crying?"

"Yes. It's so beautiful, it touches my heart."

At the show that night, I watched Brett play the guitar behind his head and do a little dance, showboating Jimi Hendrix style.

When the quartet actors gathered around a piano to harmonize on "Peace in the Valley" in perfect pitch, I started to cry, remembering the song my mother loved so much.

"Are you crying?" Bob said.

"Yes." I laughed as the spell was broken, but that is what theater and music do. They take you to a place in your mind as nothing else can.

After the show, we went for dinner and drinks.

"Mother cried during your performance," Bob said.

"Mom, you cried again?" He chuckled.

"Yes, son, I cried twice today, for cryin' out loud."

We laughed. It was so good to spend time with Brett.

I thought of a night two years before when Brett cried in frustration over his career in New York. He had been booed off the stage at the Apollo Theater's amateur night. His band consisted of one other player, his roommate, Damian.

They moved to New York together after college. Brett played guitar and keyboard, and Damian, a rapper, played drums, keyboard, and harmonica.

They wrote their songs and recorded them on video, marketing themselves online. They sold T-shirts, buttons, and CDs at their concerts and busked on the subway, until the police chased them off.

Bob and I flew in to see them play the Apollo. The house was packed, and Brett and Damian's band, Sham, came on last.

Brett's hair was long and curly, and he wore a suit. Damien's hair was cut short, and he also wore a suit. It took a few minutes to plug in and get set after they walked on stage.

They started to play a hard-rock original that Damian wrote with a long instrumental introduction. The members of the Apollo backup band looked at one another and shook their heads. Soon, the clown came on stage, blowing his horn and dancing them off while the crowd booed.

Brett and Damian were stoic outside as audience members shook their hands. One person thought they sounded good and should have been given the chance to finish their song.

"Thanks, man," Brett said as he handed him his business card. "We play the Bitter End tomorrow night. Come see us."

The Bitter End is a small, dirty, famous bar in Greenwich Village where Carol King, Bob Dylan, and other great musicians played. Brett and Damian had a one-hour slot at 10 p.m.

Brett came out wearing his signature black suit I had bought him at Macy's for his New York look.

They opened with "Gotta Get a Cat," a song Brett wrote about the mouse problem in their apartment.

"We were booed off the stage at the Apollo Theater last night. Can you believe that?" Damian said before vowing to return.

Over whiskey and chocolate cake at the crowded Hilton lobby bar with me and Bob later that night, Brett broke down and cried.

"Mom, why does New York have to be so hard?" he said. "I went to three call backs for "One Man, Two Guvnors," and I didn't get the part. Now the Apollo boos me off the stage, and I got to work dinner at the Spice Market tomorrow night. New York is so hard."

"Listen, son, suck it up," Bob said.

Brett cried more, as I drank my martini.

In the quiet of the room on the eleventh floor, Brett assured us he was okay. He picked up his acoustic guitar, played softly, and sang his newest song. Bob and I were mesmerized by his talent.

"Son, remember the song 'New York, New York'? If I can make it there, I'll make it anywhere," I said.

Brett smiled and kept singing.

"The Apollo Theater just isn't ready for your sound, son. They always pick someone to boo off the stage. It is part of their schtick. Last night it was you," I said. "Don't feel bad. You are in good company. James Brown was booed off that stage the first time he played there too, but he came back and owned the place. Hey, you got booed off the stage, but you still played the Apollo Theater. How many people can say that?"

We laughed.

That night in Manhattan came back to me, when I heard Elvis talk to Sam Phillips in *Million Dollar Quartet*.

"The Colonel had me open for Shecky Greene, and they booed me off the stage every night. I am never playing Vegas again," Elvis said. Knowing his Vegas future, the audience laughed.

Elvis persevered, and so will Brett.

"How does it feel to have your son follow in your footsteps?" Bob's brother said to me. "He looks just like you. It's like watching you on stage again."

I realized I had gone from the stage to stage mom. I did not consider my influence on Brett's choice of the stage until I saw a televised interview he did for "Rockin' Road to Dublin."

"My mom played piano and sang at music parties she hosted in our home in California. There was always music around," Brett said when asked how he got into musical theater. "When we moved to Georgia, my room was in the basement and that's where the piano was. Mom came down to practice in my room, and she would sing Patsy Cline songs so passionately. Sometimes she would open the basement door from the kitchen and sing loudly "House of the Rising Sun." It echoed down the stairwell.

Brett's interest in the stage had seemed to evolve organically. The whole family loved the theater.

"Don't give yourself too much credit," Bob said. "Kids choose their paths for many reasons. There are plenty of doctors whose children did not pursue medicine."

Brett could have been a doctor, but he chose acting.

At twenty-eight, the age I started, he has endured longer than I did, and he has had more success.

How long before he tires of being the starving artist who is only as good as his last show, having to pay rent by waiting tables between gigs? He rides on million-dollar tour buses across the country, which sounds glamorous until you realize he falls off his bunk when the bus rounds a curve.

He's a troubadour who knows the next ride will be smoother because he has something to believe in: himself.

Boater-Head

The portly man standing behind me, grunted as I stored my sweater in the overhead bin on our flight to Boston.

"That works," he said.

"Are you sitting here?" I said, taking my middle seat.

"Yes."

He tried to slip out of his coat, and his hat fell under the seat. "Dressed for Boston; I'm burning up," he said.

Sweat beaded on his forehead. As he sat down, I lowered the armrest, otherwise he would melt into me. The seat groaned, and the armrest dug into him. He picked up his hat from the floor—a flat brim straw hat with a wide ribbon band.

"I'm going to a thirty-year college class reunion, so I thought a boater would be fitting," he said, as he put the hat in the overhead bin.

"Is that what it's called?" I said.

"Yes, I do imitations of Winston Churchill wearing a bowler, though he never wore one; people expect it. Lady Astor said, 'If I were your wife, Mr. Churchill, I'd poison your tea.' Churchill replied, 'If I were your husband, I'd drink it.'"

"Good one," I said.

I opened my newspaper just wide enough to fit my seat space. Boater-head held his iPad to the end of his nose to read it. He tapped the screen, and with each tap his elbow poked my arm. He knew he was banging into me and getting closer to my left breast all the time. I raised my newspaper to block his assault.

"Oh, sorry," he said.

My husband Bob sat next to me by the window. *Maybe he should change seats with me. Large men always encroach on my space, as if I am not entitled to it by virtue of my size. Just don't touch me, and I'm fine.*

The food cart came by, and I pulled out the bagel I brought from the Sky Lounge.

"Oh, you came prepared," Boater-head said.

"Yes."

"I'd like to order a snack," he said to the flight attendant, "What do you have?"

"Look in the magazine," she said.

He opened the magazine and put it on the tip of his nose to read.

"The cheese box, please," he said, "and a Diet Coke, pretzels, and cookies."

His tray table jammed unevenly against his girth. The cheese box, pretzels, cookies, Coke can, cup of ice, laptop, cell phone, and wallet teetered there.

I knew he would spill his drink on me before the flight was over, and I was wearing white pants.

I ordered a Diet Coke and finished my bagel as fast as I could.

"Would you like me to top off your drink?" he said, "You can have some of my Diet Coke."

"No, thanks."

I was sure he would top me off soon enough.

I watched him fumble with the cheese box, opening packages, poking me with his elbow, the Diet Coke balancing next to me. As he ate each package in his cheese box, one pack of chips fell into the aisle. The passenger across the aisle picked it up.

"Oh, thank you," he said, fumbling again..

His tray table now was full of empty packages, and he topped off his Diet Coke just as turbulence bounced us around. I waited for the Coke to spill. He held it in his hand, and his wallet fell against my leg.

"You're about to lose your wallet," I said.

"Oh, thank you," he said, and let go of his Coke to grab his wallet.

Anticipating the spill, I spread napkins across my lap. I tried to close my eyes and relax, but Boater-head's tray table bothered me. I wanted to give him instructions.

Pick up your crap. Stuff it in the box, put it on the floor. Get rid of the empty can too. Finish that drink already, before you spill it on me for Christ's sake!

At last, I had to cross my legs or get a cramp, trapped in the middle seat with my tray table down, between Boater-head poking me, and my size large husband, Bob, taking up all the space to the right of me.

"I need to move this," I said to Bob. At least I could boss him around a little.

"Okay."

I stuffed my napkins and the sticky jelly package into my empty cup and placed them on the small plate. When I picked it up, everything toppled onto Boater-head's leg.

"I'm so sorry," I said.

"It's okay. No harm."

I reached down to get the jelly pack from the floor, and it stuck to my fingers which brushed against my white pants. "Damn, nice stain," I said.

The Jewish Mom

1987-1994

"Mom, is Santa Claus real?" Kristy said as we strolled down the sidewalk to the children's store, Our Gang, on Balboa Island in California.

"No," I said.

A man sitting on the bench overheard me and leapt to his feet. "Why are you telling her that?"

"Because it's true."

"But she's a little girl." He shook his head and sat down again.

Kristy was three, and I didn't know how to be a Jewish mother. Because I had converted to Judaism when I married Bob, I had no background in how to teach a Jewish child. I sounded cruel to that stranger.

One year I couldn't resist getting a small Christmas tree. The children were young, and I thought I could find a way for them not to feel left out at Christmas. Bob's parents were coming over, and I was a little concerned about what Betty might say.

She examined the tree, then chided, "You couldn't find a nicer one?"

Christmas was tough in a Jewish household. Bob didn't mind if I put up colored lights outside, but he fussed and fumed when I got a tree. I planned parties with other Jewish families on Christmas Day so it wasn't so lonely. Otherwise we went to the movies and ate Chinese food.

Christmas was a thorn in Bob's side. Sometimes I took the kids back to Georgia for the holiday and decorated Grandma Coker's tree. She could care less about a tree, but I did it for me and the children. We stored the decorations at her house while we lived in Nashville, then Mother sent them to me when we moved back to California.

Brett wrote this note to Santa when he was seven:

> "Dear Santa,
> If you are real, I would like Golden-Eye James Bond and Diddy Kong Racing on Nintendo 64. I've been good and bad, so if you don't get me anything I'll understand.
> By Brett
> PS. I think it's only my parents."

By this time, Brett was in second grade, and we had moved back to Georgia. A few Jewish families also lived in the little town of Cartersville. Most of Brett's friends were Christians. Brett wanted to let them understand how different his religion is. "Mother, what day is Christmas on?" he said.

The other boys were stunned that Brett didn't know what day Christmas was.

"December 25th."

"Is it on the same day every year?"

All the Jewish holidays fall on different days using the Jewish calendar that dates back five thousand years. Some holidays last for eight days. Brett was fascinated that Christmas was the same day every year.

I did a good job raising Jewish kids, sending them to the temple and religious school. I could have gone to class with them during their Bar and Bat Mitzvah years of training and learned along with them, but instead I read phonetic transcriptions of the Hebrew prayers. The translations also were included in the prayer books. I sometimes felt like a stranger in my own home.

One year, when the kids were in high school and college, I bought a Christmas tree. It was beautiful, decorated with colored lights and some of the old ornaments Grandma Coker had sent.

"Mom, what're you doing? We're Jewish. We don't celebrate Christmas," Kristy said.

Oh, yeah, I guess I always got the tree for me.

Even today with no children in the house, I still put up a small handmade tree with art pieces decorated in blue, the Hanukkah color. It is a very untraditional tree. Bob doesn't complain about it anymore. He gave up. The compromise was small.

"I like your Hanukkah bush," Bob's co-worker Mecca said when she came to our home for a holiday party.

Israel

In 2000, Kristy spent the summer of her tenth grade in Israel with a group from the temple. I missed her call and listened to the answering machine:

"Hey, Mom, Dad, and family. It's Kristy. I'm in Israel right now. I know this is not the best time to call, but I just can't find time to write. I'm having a great trip. It is so awesome. I'm standing at my Israeli sponsor's house in Haifa and looking out at the city. Shaina Miller and I are best friends, and we're having so much fun. I'll try to call you later today. We're going out to some clubs tonight, so tell Laura and Shayne and all my friends I said hi. I haven't written, but it takes weeks to get a letter to you, and I'll be home by then. I'll call you anyway. Okay, everyone, I love you. I'm having a great visit, and don't worry about anything. I'm being safe and cautious. Bye. I love you, Abba and Emma. Shalom."

All our children spent their tenth-grade summers in Israel on an excursion with the National Federation of Temple Youth as part of their confirmation. They flew into Cyprus and took a rickety boat ride for three days to Israel to reenact the voyage of the famous *SS Exodus*—the ship that transported forty-five hundred Jewish illegal immigrants from France to British Mandatory Palestine on July 11, 1947. Most were Holocaust survivors. The ship was taken to Haifa where other vessels were waiting to return the Jews to refugee camps in Europe.

Historians say "Exodus 1947" deepened international sympathy for the plight of Holocaust survivors and rallied support for the creation of a Jewish state. Israel was declared a state soon after, on May 14, 1948.

Five rabbis and five hundred students from temples around the country were part of Kristy's trip. In 2000 Israel was more or less peaceful after their various wars with surrounding nations.

In 1996, the year Shayne was scheduled to go, the trip was canceled. "Operation Grapes of Wrath" was a sixteen-day campaign against Lebanon, attempting to end rocket attacks on Northern Israel by Hezbollah.

The summer trips remained suspended for a few years as Israel fought various attacks from surrounding Arab countries. In 2001 when Shayne was in college, she was able to join another group for a tour after another student cancelled her reservation with Birthright Israel, the sponsor. Although sponsoring organizations were careful to protect their students who travelled to Israel, some dropped out of the programs. That year, many of the sites were closed because of Palestinian rocket and mortar attacks.

In 2005, Brett spent the summer of his tenth grade in Israel. He attended a recruitment class, and he wanted to join the IDF (Israeli Defense Forces) after high school. I didn't want my boy to go from my kitchen table to the war zone. I was determined not to finance his trip to become a warrior. Instead I offered to send him to a college study abroad in Israel.

In 2011, the day before he was to leave, the Ben-Gurion University in Be'er Shevah where he would attend, was bombed. The Hamas were lobbing rockets from Gaza into the Capital of the Negev. His trip was delayed for two weeks, and I was ready to cancel it. After much family discussion and talks with the program directors, the portion of the curriculum that included a two-week stay at Hatzerim kibbutz was suspended because it was too close to the hostilities in Gaza. The rest of the program was maintained, and we let him go.

I was the only one in the family who had not been to Israel. I wanted to see the country that intrigued my family and became the cornerstone to the Jewish religion, and many other religions, for that matter.

To satisfy my curiosity, Bob and I joined Brett for Spring Break and Passover. I was not comfortable navigating a war-torn country where I did not speak the language. Though most Israeli's speak English, not all do. We booked a private tour, and the cautious guide drove us to the famous sites. Many were closed for Passover, and most of the public transportation was shut down for the sacred holiday. Brett took a private car to meet us at our hotel in Tel Aviv.

When we toured Old Jerusalem and the Wailing Wall of the old temple, I realized the importance this city has to many cultures. It is divided into four quarters: The Jewish Quarter, The Armenian Quarter, The Christian Quarter, and The Muslim Quarter. People enter the walled city through one of seven gates.

At the Wailing Wall, the shawl I had purchased for the occasion slipped from my shoulders, exposing them. A local woman asked me to please replace my shawl, since it is customary for women to cover themselves at the wall. I pulled my garment back into place, and the woman thanked me, then held out her hand to beg for money. I had none to give her but turned back to the wall for a prayer that included her.

During our tour, the days came for not only Passover, but also Easter, and we were in the midst of a cultural mélange. We stood by while a Greek Orthodox parade passed with uniformed children playing instruments. The discordant Muslim call to prayer rang out across the city from the mosque. We ate lunch in the Arab Market, one of the best meals I ever had, of lamb, humus, and baba ganoush. For dinner on the Jewish side of the city, we dined on chickpea shawarma and falafel pitas.

Peace exists somewhat in Old Jerusalem, with these many cultures enjoying their claim to the city, but armed soldiers signal when you enter the Jewish side of town where homes of the Ultra-Orthodox Jewish families line its narrow alleyways. The Muslim Quarter is a huge contrast to the Jewish Quarter. Its streets are busier and more crowded with vendors in the famous Shuk selling all varieties of products. The locals go about their business, kids play in the street, and men sit in cafes, smoking hookah.

I never imagined how small the country is. While touring the Golan Heights, the site of the Six Day War against Syria in 1967, I realized the country of Syria was just across the street behind the fence.

When Bob and I toured Brett's school, built of heavy concrete with small windows like a bunker, Brett showed me the hole in the ground where the low-range Grad rocket fired by Palestinian terrorists landed before he arrived on campus. The senior students joked about being a grad with a Grad rocket, and they even made a t-shirt. These rockets could reach only fifty miles, but they were deadly when they landed. Brett's school was within range. The IDF quickly put an end to the skirmish.

Armed guards stood outside movie theaters and shopping malls, and off-duty soldiers went to the beach or the bar with an M-16 slung over their shoulders. I tried to enter the mall a few minutes before it opened, and a guard blocked my path. At Shabbat dinner in the restaurant of our hotel, a soldier dressed in shorts relaxed, but the M-16 never left his arm.

As we drove across the country on our tour, large military trucks passed us with 'MADE IN THE USA' stamped in large letters across the back. As if to say, 'the USA has our back.' Many of the young people we met at the university or on our tour were thrilled to talk to us about the United States. They hoped to visit one day.

U.S. citizens are welcomed in Israel and treated well. Except for all the armed guards, at times I felt I was visiting another state in our country. At the five-star Scots Hotel, St. Andrew's Galilee in Tiberias, where we stayed, I never got to enjoy a beautiful pool because our tour left at nine in the morning and returned at five. The pool closed every day at five o'clock.

At the end of a day of touring, I went to the hotel clerk to see if he could please leave the pool open for another hour so I could swim. He said no, and I asked him why.

"Madam," he said, "this is Israel.

From Istanbul with Love

The sunlight streaked across room 505 of the Istanbul Hilton, and Kristy pulled the pillow over her face to keep out the light.

"Your dad and I are going downstairs for breakfast," I said. "You have twenty minutes to get dressed."

Kristy had no appetite at this hour. In the bathroom, she washed her face and brushed her teeth, no time for a shower. She gazed into the mirror and wiped the makeup from beneath her eyes with cold crème. "God."

Her long brown hair tangled to her shoulders, and her green eyes, slightly blood shot, stared back at her. Wearing a halter top over her ample breasts and a pair of leggings, she was ready. With her jacket in hand, she followed us out.

"Cuppa Cuppa," the elevator voiced in Turkish.

"Cuppa Cuppa," Kristy said. "I wonder what that means."

Bob and I planned to meet our friends Karen and Andrew in Istanbul. Bob didn't want to go, even though I talked about it for years.

"I've always wanted to see the Hagia Sophia ever since I studied about it in college," I had told him. "Remember when we were in Greece? I wanted to go to Istanbul, but it made the trip too long."

"I have no interest in Istanbul," Bob said.

"Your grandfather was from there."

"That's his problem."

"Aren't you interested in seeing where you hail from?"

"I hail from Nashville. I'll go there with you. Besides, I need to plan a trip to California to see my brother."

Bob saw there was no way to talk me out of this, and he reluctantly agreed to go. Kristy learned about the trip when she called home.

"Can I go?"

Bob considered letting Kristy go in his place, but he knew I would be disappointed. "Can you get the days off from work?"

She had arranged it.

At 8:00 a.m., the tour bus pulled into the Hilton circle drive. We boarded and sat in the back looking out the dirty windows for our first view of Istanbul.

"Is that the Blue Mosque?" Kristy said.

But there are many mosques in Istanbul.

The bus picked up more passengers and bounced through the crowded streets with horns honking, and pedestrians scurrying between cars. An overloaded tram weaved through the city on rails.

"That's the public transportation Karen mentioned," I told Bob. "We might use it next time."

Though I preferred a guided tour picking me up at the hotel, feeding me lunch, and dropping me back. I didn't want to rely on my wits in a foreign country of Turkish-speaking people to help me navigate the city. I would wait for Karen to direct us on the tram.

The tour bus made its first stop. "We will be walking now. Bring all your belongings off the bus," the guide said.

I looked down at my beige, pointed-toed, patent leather flats from Bloomingdale's, beautiful, but not good for walking long distances. I had dressed up for my first tour of Istanbul and the Hagia Sophia.

We walked the Hippodrome where ancient chariots once ran, but now it is a large space with obelisks thousands of years old. I had to go to the bathroom, and the tour guide directed me around the building. I had ten minutes before the tour resumed, and I followed a group of people. But that couldn't be right. They were going into a large building so I turned around to discover a small building with a man inside the window.

"Toilet?" I said.

"One lira." He pointed downstairs.

I handed him a coin and walked down the narrow stairs into a small bathroom with no paper and no water to wash my hands. European women stood complaining in front of the mirror. I rushed past them, taking care of business, and hurried back upstairs before the smell got to me. *What did I expect for one lira?*

With each stop, the tour guide spoke English with a heavy accent and held up a flag to follow him through the bustling city. At the Blue Mosque, Bob's headphones didn't work. I weaved my way to the guide, who tested them as he continued speaking on the tour.

"They don't work," he said.

"Yeah, I know," I said.

"I don't need them," Bob said.

"Yes, you do, this is great information."

The tour guide brought Bob a new headset as we readied ourselves to enter the Blue Mosque. Kristy and I draped our scarves over our heads. Bob, wearing shorts, tied a blue cloth at his waist to cover his legs. We took off our shoes, put them in plastic bags, and walked barefoot on the beautiful, plush carpet of the Blue Mosque.

"It smells like feet in here," Kristy said.

But in fact, there are ancient foot washing stations built alongside the mosques for those going to pray rather than tour. This practice of humility is also found in Christianity.

Inside the Blue Mosque, mosaic tiles adorned the many domes in the main sanctuary with windows shaped into arches to light the building. A brilliant chandelier twinkled with light bulbs twisted into oblong shapes. The mosque is still used for religious purposes and closed to tourists on those days.

Kristy looked like she belonged in the mosque. You could see the Turkish heritage in her face. Draped in her shawl, she could pass for a local girl, though a perfect blend of Bob and me. Bob is tall, dark, and handsome, and Kristy has inherited my green eyes but not my red hair that peeked out from my shawl. Kristy garnered the attention of everyone in the room when she entered. At 5'10" she towered over most people in Istanbul except her father, who was 6'2".

Before immigrating to the U.S., Bob's grandfather grew up in Izmir near Istanbul, and Friday night we planned to meet Bob's cousins for the first time for services in the Jewish Temple in Ataköy.

"Do we have to get together with your cousins Friday night?" I said. "That's the first night Karen and Andrew are available for dinner after his conference."

"Hey, you wanted me to come on this trip, so I contacted my cousins through Facebook. While we're looking at all these mosques, I'd like to see a synagogue in this country and go to services."

"What if it's dangerous? Why are we attracting attention to ourselves?"

"Well, it might be. We have to bring our passports, and my cousin Izzit will meet us there. We can't get in otherwise. I should also tell you something else."

"What?"

"The synagogue we're going to was bombed twenty-five years ago, killing seventy-five people."

"Jesus, Bob, what the fuck?"

"It's okay. That was twenty-five years ago, a bunch of radicals. Things are different now."

"How do you know?"

"I emailed Izzit's wife, Cella. You know Uncle Sol's daughter, Alizah, lived here for two years."

"Yeah, did she go to the temple when she was here?"

"Yes, in fact she gave me Izzit's contact information."

"Great," I said. "Why do you have to be so religious?"

Bob smiled at this. He knew forty years ago, when I converted to Judaism and reared our three children in the Jewish faith, I had deep respect for his religion, though inconvenient sometimes.

"Friday night is services, and they have invited us to their home afterwards for a kosher meal," Bob said. "Izzit keeps kosher. Cella asked if I did."

"No, we don't keep kosher. We hardly ever go to temple, now that the kids are grown," I said.

***

At Hagia Sophia, the construction scaffolding contrasted with the ancient building, which was dark with stained glass windows reflecting the light. The architecture was similar to that of the Blue Mosque, with its cupola shaped windows pouring daylight into each dome. One of the archways still held ancient mosaic tiles of the original ceiling from the sixth century.

I stood in silence, mesmerized by the artful display of the oldest part of the temple, trying to absorb the history, remembering my studies of Constantinople and the Ottoman Empire.

Gilded doorways and vaults accentuate the central room where Eastern Orthodox services were once held, but today the mosque is a museum. Golden friezes of the Christ Child, Mary, and the Wise Men adorn the room. Turkish lettered discs extoll the many centuries of history.

"I need to find a bathroom," Bob said.

"Okay, take one lira. We'll meet you back here."

Kristy and I walked up the stone ramp to the second-floor gift shop.

"Can you imagine what this place was like during the Ottoman Empire?" I said. "Women sat up here during services."

"It's not that different in the Jewish religion today, Mom, if you're Orthodox," Kristy said.

"True. It's amazing how similar the religions are, and I think it's because they are both so ancient and come from the same region. Your dad's grandpa immigrated to the U.S. from Izmir. His last name was Moskowitz. He changed it once he got to New York, but look, here we are in a mosque. He probably came from the mosque with a name like that. Back in the sixth century, maybe the religions had more in common than now."

"Was his first name Fieval? Was he a mouse?" Kristy said.

I laughed. "Yes, he was a mouse—Fieval Moskowitz. You remember the movie."

"You should be a historian, Mom." Kristy giggled.

"I do enjoy research, but this seems obvious. Where's your dad? It's time to meet the tour." I touched the display case. "I like this necklace. We've got to go. I hope Karen will bring us back here."

The next stop, Grand Bazaar, where a cavern of retailers hawked their wares: leather, silk, rugs, shoes, pashmina, and trinkets. The cacophony of people and goods produced a high energy.

"I'm going to walk around," Kristy said. "I'll catch up with you all later."

"Okay. Remember we have to meet at Gate One at one o'clock," I said.

Kristy disappeared into the crowd.

"Let's stay on the main street," I said. "I'm afraid I'll get lost on the side streets."

"Fine. This looks like a bunch of crap anyway," Bob said.
"I might want a pashmina."

***

Kristy wandered down a side street and bought a few bracelets, maybe she would give one to her older sister Shayne. Kristy wanted to come on this trip alone without Shayne or her younger brother Brett. The whole family had just returned from an Alaskan cruise that she enjoyed, but with everyone along she just blended in with the other two. Kristy wanted her own experience without their influence.

I had agreed, since herding three people on tours was easier than five.

Kristy turned down another street to the leather store. The tour only allowed forty-five minutes to shop. Not enough time for this large place.

"Come inside, pretty lady. Have some tea," a shop owner called to her.

She strolled inside and sat on a cowhide covered stool enjoying the hot tea. She then tried on a pair of handmade leather shoes which she purchased. Outside, she retraced her steps, then realized she was lost. As merchants called out to her, she began to sweat, looking at the time fleeting away on her cell phone that did not work in this city.

A handsome young man with dark hair and eyes, wearing a wrinkled shirt, saw her frightened face and greeted her. "Can I help you?"

"I'm lost. I need to get back to Gate One."

"Follow me."

Unsure where he might take her, nothing looked familiar as she kept walking. He glanced back at her and took her hand, pulling her along with authority. She tried to trust him and the chaos around her. The crowds grew thicker.

Now, time to meet the tour guide, she panicked and let go of the strange hand, running in the opposite direction. He chased after her.

"Don't be afraid. I will help you. My name is Piton. I own the Pashmina shop. I will help you," he said again.

Kristy ran through the alley, frightened.

Merchants called out to her, "Come inside," and the sound got louder and more garbled in her ears. She turned another corner and saw the entrance to Gate One and hurried toward it.

"Goodbye, beautiful, I love you," Piton shouted.

"I got lost back there," Kristy said as she joined the group.

"Easy to do with those side streets," I said. "We stayed on the main road so we could make it back in time."

The impatient tour guide called to everyone to keep up as we crossed the narrow, cobbled streets to our lunch stop. Kristy, tall enough to see over the heads, kept the guide in her sights. The group filed down the stairs of a small, noisy restaurant to their reserved table. The smell of smoked lamb with cumin and nutmeg wafted through the air.

The young waiter, with dark hair that swept into his brown eyes, approached Kristy first.

"I'd like a beer, please," she said.

He lingered there, watching Kristy as he took orders all around.

The other guests at the table included a couple from India traveling with their son, and two couples from Kuwait, who vacation in Istanbul often, as it is a short flight.

The waiter returned with drinks teetering on his tray. He took a closer look at Kristy and dropped her glass of beer. Glass showered everyone. Kristy laughed, and the waiter's face reddened.

"Could we get another lavash?" I said. "I'm afraid we have glass in this one."

The waiter ducked out of sight.

"Mom, don't be so hard on the waiter," Kristy said. "He's cute,"

"Still, I don't want to eat glass—not sure travel insurance covers that."

The waiter never came back with more bread.

After lunch the tour guide directed everyone to the Topkapi Palace for a two hour do-it-yourself walkabout. The palace has a long history of sultans, and today serves as a large museum beautifully landscaped with colorful flowers and water features. By now, my shoes had rubbed blisters, and I carried them and walked barefoot trying to stay in the cool grass. The palace covered two blocks, and people lined up for the various exhibits, including the crown jewels and the haram house of the sultan. The walls overlooked the Bosporus Strait with its many islands.

In the circumcision hall, Bob said, "Do you think the Sultan was Jewish?"

But in fact, circumcision is a religious tradition of Islam for cleanliness and purity. There were ceremonies for the princes-sons of Sultan Ahmet III 1703-1730. In the Jewish religion, boys are circumcised when they are eight days old.

Later, when we toured with Karen and Andrew, we saw young boys on the grounds of the mosques, eating ice cream cones, dressed in their ceremonial white suits with a yellow feathered hat, waiting for their rite of passage. Karen would explain that the Muslims wait until the boys are eight years old, and it is more painful, so the boys are not promiscuous and regard sex with more respect.

"Yeah, while Jewish boys screw around at a very early age." Bob laughed. "At least they gave them ice cream before."

I felt pangs of sadness for the young boys, as I remembered my son Brett's circumcision as an infant. I didn't want him to feel pain. Even though the Moyle assured me he would not, I had insisted he have a Novocain shot to his penis to numb it.

I watched the needle tip insert into the tiny vein that ran along the top of Brett's penis. He let out a little cry then stifled into a sniffle. After the wine and food celebration with family and friends, I retired upstairs to the baby's room to nurse him for my comfort as well as his.

The Moyle came up to check on Brett one more time before he left. He had opened Brett's diaper to inspect the angry red penis.

"It looks good."

***

The next night a dinner cruise was on the itinerary. Buses lined up at the Hilton to transport tourists to various destinations. The lobby was full of people waiting for their conveyance. The concierge would call us when our bus arrived. I ordered a martini at the bar, and Kristy ordered a gin and tonic. Bob had a glass of wine. Soon the bus arrived, and we boarded along with other tourists to head to the port.

On the Bosporus dinner cruise, the small boat was filled to capacity with tables surrounding a small stage, and diners from different countries. Turkish dancers from various regions performed. A belly dancer took the stage, gyrating her large hips and shapely breasts. She approached Bob, undulating in front of him. He stuffed twenty lira into her bra, and she dragged him onto the stage. I jumped up to take pictures.

"Please sit down. You are blocking the view of the guests at the tables," the waiter growled.

I waved him off and continued photographing. The waiter tried to escort me back to my seat, but I elbowed him away. As the belly dancer shimmied against Bob, I pushed my way onto the stage, standing in front of the entertainer in a challenge. The dancer moved in close, and I returned her erotic moves as Bob watched. Soon we both surrounded him dancing in harmony for his pleasure, and the audience applauded.

A man from another table approached Kristy. "The belly dancer is on the floor, but all I can see is you," he said in a strong Irish brogue.

Kristy, accustomed to the attention, gave him a demure smile.

As the cruise boat motored down the Bosporus, everyone enjoyed dinner. A young couple from Iraq sat across from Kristy. The woman wore a beautiful pink flowered hijab that matched her pink jacket.

"I love your hijab," Kristy said. "What's your name?"

"Raheem," she said. "We just got married. This is our honeymoon."

"Istanbul is beautiful. This is my first time here," Kristy said. "I lived in Dubai for two years and flew for Emirates Airline. I wore a hijab for my uniform."

"I hear Dubai can be very strict with Muslim customs. Were you afraid living there?"

"Well, I had to get a new passport, when I entered the country, because of a stamp from Israel on my old passport. Dubai will not let you in the country, if you have visited Israel. I kept a low profile with my Western customs and tried not to be disrespectful. I did not kiss my boyfriend in public, and I dressed conservatively."

Kristy thought back to her interview with Emirates Air.

***

"Okay, Kristy, I just need a copy of your diploma from The University of Georgia, and you can begin class next month. I have one more question: What is your religious preference?" the interviewer said.

Kristy knew this could be a deal breaker, so she hesitated before she answered. "I am Jewish, but my grandmother is Christian."

The interviewer paused a moment. "Let's put down Christian."

Kristy agreed, but she didn't feel good about denying her religion.

"Mom, everything I said was true," she told me later, when she called home after the interview.

"I know. It's hard to be a Jewish girl named Kristy," I said, "but I think it speaks to your heritage. There is a Christian influence."

***

Raheem interrupted Kristy's thoughts. "Did you like Dubai?"

"I loved it," Kristy said. "My boyfriend was an engineer, and when I graduated from the University of Georgia, I moved with him to Dubai. He had a two-year contract with Haliburton to build highrises there."

"This is the first time I have left my country. We move to Seattle, and my husband will work for Boeing," Raheem said.

"Do you worry about living in the U.S.?"

"Yes, I do, but like you, I will try to keep a low profile," Raheem said.

"Yes, good advice, although America can be very tolerant. How old are you?"

"Twenty-four," Raheem said. "How old are you?"

"Thirty."

"You look so fresh.

Kristy laughed. "Thanks."

"Where do you live now?" Raheem said.

"I live in Miami. I'm in public relations."

"I'm an engineer, and I plan to find a job in Seattle," Raheem said. Her husband smiled.

Another couple from Kuwait sat beside Kristy.

"I heard you talking about Dubai. I am an architect, and I designed the Burg Khalifa along with Ski Dubai.

"Oh, yes. I know them both very well. The air at Ski Dubai was so cold,

I thought my hands would fall off, but I guess they have to keep it freezing in that desert," Kristy said. "I lived in the Burg Khalifa,"

"My children live in New York so I get to the U.S. often. I am also designing a building in New York." He leaned in. "At the Hilton, I saw you get on the bus with your drink in your hand, and I knew you were well travelled. I made sure we sat at your table tonight. Maybe we can work together on a project."

Kristy understood the meaning of this proposal and got up to join the dancers as the DJ played songs from each country. Soon the dance floor filled with people swinging to the music. The air thickened, and Kristy went out on the aft deck to cool off. She bummed a cigarette from a young man with blond hair wearing a sweatshirt.

"Where are you from?" she said.

"Croatia. You are American, right?"

"Yes. How did you know?"

"Americans are easily distinguished by their clothes."

"I bought this outfit in Paris."

He stepped closer and whispered, "I would love to kiss you."

Kristy took one more drag off her cigarette and flicked it over the side. "Peace out," she said and strolled back inside.

On the bus ride back to the Hilton, young people packed the streets, walking, stopping traffic—more pedestrians than vehicles on a Saturday night in Istanbul. Kristy sat up front and looked back at us and mouthed, 'I'm going out tonight.'

She smiled with beautiful white teeth. That meant trouble.

Back in our room at 12:30 a.m., Kristy texted her friend, Sydney, an ex-pat living there for two years now. "Let's go out."

"I just got in. I'm tired, but go to Gizli Bahce in Balik Pazar (fish market) or Peyote," she texted back.

When Kristy told me her plans, I said, "I don't think you should go out alone. Your phone only works with Wi-Fi and the battery is low. Just go to bed. It's late. We have a big day rug shopping with Karen and Andrew tomorrow."

"Mom, did you see all those people my age? The night is young. I'm thirty, and I've lived in a Middle Eastern country. I know how to take care of myself."

She brushed her flowing mane of hair, put on lipstick, and grabbed her yellow coat. "I'll be back in a couple of hours. Don't worry."

She walked out the door, her cowboy booties clomping with each step, and pressed the button to the elevator.

"Cuppa! Cuppa!" the elevator voiced.

"That's right, baby, Cuppa! Cuppa! Let's get out of here," she said, as she entered the elevator.

In the lobby, she talked to the front desk clerk. "Where should I go for a drink and some entertainment?"

"Taksim Square. Just walk left outside the hotel for about fifteen minutes. Follow the crowd to Istiklal Caddesi."

***

I tried to busy myself with the machinations of a bedtime ritual, but a furrowed brow stared back at me in the mirror. How could I sleep while my lovely daughter, who has had too much to drink, is out alone in an Arab country? A Jewish girl alone on the streets of Istanbul, looking for adventure with kids her age on a Saturday night. I tried to take heart that Sydney had recommended places to go, but at 1:00 a.m., it felt wrong.

"Bob, I'm worried. She doesn't understand. This is not the U.S."

"You told her not to go. That's all you can do." Bob went to bed.

As a flight attendant in my youth, traveling the world and sometimes alone in a foreign city, I understood Kristy but was discomfited by my imagination. I got into bed conjuring positive thoughts that Kristy, much older than I was at that stage in my life, had more confidence in an Arab country. I closed my eyes, knowing that when I woke up, Kristy would be in her roll-away bed.

I slept. Bob snored.

***

With no trouble, Kristy found Taksim Square as she followed the people teeming past the retail stores now closed. When she reached the wide open concrete expanse of the Square adjoining Gezi Park, an antique tram ran along the avenue dividing the crowd from its path. After a few minutes walking past bars and restaurants, a bar promoter approached her.

"Come inside the Address. I will buy your first drink."

Having lived in Las Vegas and Miami, Kristy was familiar with this scene and felt comfortable walking inside. He sat her at a table, brought her a beer, and opened it in front of her. Then he went back outside. The rap music thumped loudly, and Kristy enjoyed the sights and sounds of the Address. Two men sat at the table next to her and right away joined her.

"I am Bilal, and this is Ahmed. Where are you from?

"Miami."

"An American. Would you like to dance?"

The three of them danced and drank beer for the next two hours. A whiff of Bilal's fragrance, when he held her close, smelled sweet with a deeper note of spice.

"I like your cologne. You smell better than I do," Kristy said.

Bilal inhaled her hair and kissed her temple.

They embraced in time to the music for a sexy dance.

Ahmed joined another group of young people dancing to the loud music. Bilal and Kristy made out on the dance floor before returning to the table for a drink. Ahmed came over.

"I'm taking off. Nice to meet you, Kristy," he said.

"We're leaving, too. Let's go to Sokak Cafe and get some food," Bilal said.

"Would you like to come to my apartment first, for a smoke? It's just down the street." Ahmed said.

At Ahmed's apartment they smoked a joint and listened to more music. They sat on a worn couch with frayed arms. Ahmed's computer was connected to powerful speakers. Synthesized remixed music played over and over.

"What is your apartment like in Miami?"

"Small like this one. It's one room with a bed, a couch, and a small kitchen that has a microwave and no oven. The refrigerator is so close to the wall it's hard to open."

"Is Miami expensive?"

"Yes."

"Istanbul is, too. I work for my father in the rug business. What do you do?"

"Public relations."

"My father owns a retail shop on the square. I work with him," Bilal said.

"Can you make good money in public relations?" Ahmed said.

"A little… I love this song," Kristy said, as she got up and swayed to the music.

"Let's go to Otanlik. There is a DJ starting there tonight. Do you like electronic music?"

"Yes, we call it house music." Kristy pulled on her coat.

The three of them walked arm and arm down Istiklal Cadessi. Syrian street children slept in the trash strewn doorways and looked up from their slumber. They would beg for food again at first light.

***

I awoke at 4:30 a.m. Kristy's bed was empty. I opened the door to the hall. Vacant. I looked out the window to the Bosporus and the street below. The German Shepherd on the rooftop of the bar across the street, who barked to the music only a few hours ago, now slept. The streets, teeming with humanity earlier, were empty. I opened the balcony door and listened for Kristy's boots. No sound.

"Kristy!" I called into the darkness, like I did when she was a little girl.

"Judy!" Bob awoke with a jerk. "What the hell?"

"Kristy is still not back. I'm worried. It's five in the morning. Where is she?" I paced the room. "She was always the independent one who took care of herself and didn't call on me for anything. She solved her problems on her own."

I sat on her rollaway bed. "I should have paid more attention to her, but she was the middle child. I just swept her along with the other two."

"Would you stop?" Bob said. "Get hold of yourself. She'll be back. You were a good mother." His voice softened. "Look, you invited her on this trip. Now, I wish you hadn't. She's a pain in the ass,"

"What should we do?"

Bob got up. "There's nothing we can do. Do you want me to go find her?"

"Yes."

He went into the bathroom. I dialed Sydney on the house phone and left a message, 'Kristy is still not back. I'm worried. What should I do?'

Sydney would not answer at that hour, but I had to do something.

Bob climbed back in bed. *What could I do?* I lay down, but my eyes would not close, and my mind raced.

***

An hour later, Bilal's BMW entered the Hilton property, and armed guards stopped the car and asked Bilal to lower the window.

"What is your business here?" the soldier barked.

"I am dropping off a guest." Bilal showed his ID.

The guard shined his flashlight onto Kristy, who also showed her ID. He then motioned for the car to be inspected for a bomb. Another guard walked around the car with a device shaped like a wand that examined the bottom of the car before waving them through.

Bilal parked in the circle drive of the Hilton and gazed at Kristy. "I am so happy I met you. Can I see you again?"

"I'm supposed to go rug shopping with my parents today."

"I will call you."

"Text me. My phone doesn't work in this country. I've got to go."

***

At 5:50 a.m., Kristy inserted her key to room 505.

"Kristy, is that you?" I sat up.

"Yeah, Mom."

"Where have you been?"

"I went out to a club dancing with some people. Then we got some food."

"Clubs stay open this late?"

"Yeah, Mom. They do. I'm fine. Sorry to worry you."
"Well I'm glad you're here, but I got no sleep last night."
Bob rolled out of bed. "I'm going to the gym."

The Call to Prayer

The hotel phone jangled, and I answered in a hoarse voice. "Hello?"
"Kristy?"
"No."
"Judy, is that you?"
"Yes."
"You sound like a little girl," Karen said.
"What time is it?"
"Nine. I'm glad I finally got you. I picked up your message on the room phone," Karen said. "It costs me fifteen dollars to call you back."
"My phone doesn't work in this country except to text with Wi-Fi. I had to call your hotel. It's the only way I could leave a message," I told her. "I knew you were out, and you had texted me that you were turning off your texts and using voice calls. I can't do that. I have to use the WhatsApp."
"Okay, sorry, I have AT&T. It works everywhere. I thought you did, too. We'll use text. Andrew met with the Ambassador last night. I saw him later at a reception. Interesting night with the politicians," Karen said in a chatty tone.
"I bet," I said. "Andrew hangs out with some pretty high-ranking people here."
"Yeah, that's why we're here every two years. His conference is all about the warring nations surrounding Turkey. Andrew offers his expertise as the former Air Force General in charge of Special Operations. It's what he does, now that he's retired. He's on the board of many military organizations. He travels constantly, but get up, girl. We're going rug shopping. That's why I'm here."
Karen talked nonstop. "I love this place for shopping. We'll go to your guy first. I want to see what you picked out yesterday at the Grand Bazaar, then we'll go to my guy. His warehouse looks like the Marigold Hotel. Did

you see that movie?"

"Yes. What time do you want to go?"

"I'm ordering the car now. How's ten?"

I surveyed the room and remembered last night. "Can we make it 10:30? Bob's in the gym. I'm jumping in the shower, then I need coffee."

"Okay. I'll text you."

At 10:15, Karen and Andrew pulled into the Hilton driveway in their private car. Andrew climbed out first and gave everyone a hug. The General's blond hair caught the sunlight as he towered over everyone. Karen rolled out next. Short and a little overweight, she had a new hairdo—lighter brown to hide the gray.

I remembered her as a twenty-one-year-old. We flew for United Airlines back in the '70s and travelled together to Europe and South America. We each got married two weeks apart and have continued meeting each other with our husbands in exotic places such as Tuscany, Hawaii, and now Istanbul.

Everyone piled into the Mercedes SUV facing each other, and the conversation bounced around as all of us talked about our experiences in Istanbul.

"You look great, Karen. How long has it been since we got together?" I said.

"Four years ago in Tuscany, Judy. You look the same. Bob, you always look fit. You still go to the gym every day?"

"Yes."

Karen looked at Bob's tanned legs exposed by his shorts. "Do you shave your legs?"

"No."

"It looks like you do."

"Hair doesn't grow there." Bob laughed.

"Did you meet your cousins?" Andrew said.

"Yes," Bob said. "On Friday we went to services at their Temple in Ataköy, then we went to their home for a kosher meal."

I studied the mosque covered landscape and thought back to the night with Bob's family.

***

The cab pulled up to the curb of Temple Ataköy. We exited and looked at the plain-faced building.

"Is this it?" I said.

"I think so."

"Where's your cousin?" I glanced around.

"He'll be here. Let's go inside."

The door was locked. Bob rang the bell. A camera scanned us, and the door opened. An armed guard stood in the doorway.

"We're here for services," Bob said. "We're meeting our cousin, Izzit Desmonda."

The guard looked us over. "Passports."

We handed over our passports, and he took them and closed the heavy metal door.

"Great. Do we get our passports back?" I said.

"Just wait."

"Where's your cousin?"

"He'll be here."

"The security is tight here, Mom," Kristy said. "That's good."

The door opened, and the guard motioned for us to come inside. We walked into the empty building where a few men were meeting in the sanctuary. We strolled around the lobby, looking at pictures, when the Rabbi came out and greeted us.

"Welcome to Ataköy," he said.

Bob introduced us. "We are visiting from the U.S., and my cousin, Izzit Desmonda, invited us to meet him at the Temple tonight."

"Yes, of course. He told me to expect you. Make yourselves at home. Not many people come to the Friday night service. More come on Saturday morning, but there will be a few people here. You wife and daughter may go upstairs for the service. You come inside the sanctuary with Izzit when he arrives."

We took the stairs to the balcony. On a bookcase, we found little hats with ribbons that tie under the chin. We put them on and laughed, taking pictures.

"Are we allowed to take pictures?" I said.

"I don't know. Do it without being noticed," Kristy said.

We sat in the front row of the balcony alone, as a dozen men came into the sanctuary below. Bob and Izzit sat in the third row, as the Rabbi took the pulpit, and the service began.

I took a few pictures of the sanctuary when all the men below turn together in a ceremony, and I was caught photographing them. One man saw me and clapped his hands and motioned to me with an angry shrug.

I put my phone away. "Are we getting arrested?"

"I don't know, Mom. Cool it," Kristy said.

The congregants exited the Temple, and Bob introduced us to Izzit.

"We've heard so much about you. I can't believe Bob has cousins in this country," I said.

"Yes. It was a large family of nine siblings from here. Many immigrated to Argentina and Europe or the U.S. Cella's grandpa stayed here. Let's go to my house and meet Cella and our baby girl. My parents will be there. They speak English. Cella's father will be there. He speaks French but no English. Do you speak French?"

"Un peu," I said.

"Our families are very excited to meet cousins from the U.S. Dinner should be ready," Izzit said as we walked to the cabs.

In the Desmonda home, the table was set with food, and many family members gathered around for the meal. Cella said the blessing over the wine, and the table was abuzz with conversation. With each course, clean plates were set in the kosher tradition.

"Kristy, do you have a boyfriend?" Cella said.

"I'm not going with anyone now."

"How old are you?"

"Thirty."

"I didn't get married until I was thirty-eight, and Ilya was born last year, so it will happen for you, too. People seem to worry when they turn thirty, but until the right person comes along, it takes time," Cella said.

***

My attention returned to the General's car.

"They took our passports at the Temple door. Kristy and Judy had to sit in the balcony," Bob said.

"Are they Orthodox?" Karen said.

"No. Conservative."

"I thought they only separate the women in the Orthodox," Karen said.

"The whole country is Orthodox," I said. "Kristy and I were the only women there Friday night. I took a picture of the men below and one guy saw me and clapped his hands at me. He gave me a 'what the fuck' look. I thought we would be arrested when we came down, but no one really cared except him. We walked through Ataköy to find a cab. The streets were mobbed with cars and people. You take your life in your hand, when you cross a street. I wore high heels and held onto Izzit's arm to keep from falling on the cobblestones."

I felt Bob's eyes on me. "They had the most beautiful silver wine service shaped like a mountain," I continued. "After the blessing, Izzit poured a glass of wine onto the mountain. There were rivers cut into the silver, and the wine trickled down and filled the glasses encircled at the bottom." I said. "Very dramatic. We enjoyed goat's milk ice cream and fruit for dessert."

Karen studied Kristy. "How are you enjoying Istanbul?"

"I love it," Kristy said.

"Kristy stayed out all night." I said.

"Pete did that to me in Paris last year. Worried me to death. We're going to an air show next month in Paris. You guys should come, too.

"I'll go." Kristy said.

"Yes. You and Pete could hang out. You're the same age."

"I remember Pete Let's go, Mom."

"Judy, we did the same thing when we were flight attendants: staying out all night in every country we visited."

"Yes, we did."

"But the world seemed a lot safer in the '70s,"

"It really wasn't, Karen. You just didn't know any better. I was dropping bombs on Vietnam in the '70s," Andrew said.

"Yeah, and Fort Polk, Louisiana, was no picnic either." Bob chuckled.

The SUV parked, and everyone got out, as a discordant, Arabic chant in a minor key rang out over the loudspeaker from a nearby mosque.

"Hear that? The Muslim Call to Prayer. It goes off every five hours, and all the Islamic get out their prayer rugs and face the East to Saudi Arabia," Karen said.

"It sounds like the shofar warming up on Rosh Hashanah morning," Bob said.

"Is that right?" Andrew said.

Bob nodded. "A little. Very similar tune."

"Let's go." Karen waved us forward. "Our driver will stay here, so we can bring our shopping back to the car."

We entered The Grand Bazaar, where we had toured two days before. I had found a rug outside Gate One at the Istanbul Handicraft Center. I talked to Abraham, who owned the store, and he brought out the rug I had chosen.

"I bought rugs here on my last trip," Karen said, "but I don't recognize who I worked with."

"Well, I could line all my employees up for you," Abraham said.

Bob studied the rug. "Do you think Buck will like it? You know he's going to lie on it." Clearly Bob didn't want to pay much for a rug the dog would take over.

"Let's go to my other rug man," Karen whispered to me. "Abraham sounds smug. You'll like Ramadan."

"Is that his name?"

"Yes."

"Like the fasting holiday?"

Karen nodded.

"Judy, do you want the rug?" Bob said.

"Let's keep looking."

"I don't know why, if this is the one you like." Bob did not relish more rug shopping.

Kristy hung back, looking at the jewelry. She would let us parents work this out. Abraham picked up the rug. Karen and I headed for the door. Bob dragged his feet as he followed.

Down the busy street, we turned the corner as the Marigold Hotel look-alike stood in front of us. Men sat in straight back chairs smoking cigarettes, drinking Turkish coffee, and playing backgammon in front of the leather goods store. Andrew and Karen walked up the stairs to the second floor.

"Watch your step." Karen pointed down. "These old stairs are slippery,"

The marble stairs had depressed centers, making them uneven from thousands of years of feet tramping there. A balcony surrounded the second floor. The carved wooden balustrades had a pattern of spools painted red and white. The saw-cut, concrete floor had green and white painted squares, resembling tiles. A narrow column of pipe held up the balcony of each floor. Sunlight reflected onto the three levels through a glass rooftop. Retail stores lined the balcony, offering lamps, food, jewelry, and pashmina among other things.

"Hello, Ramadan. I brought my friends." Karen said, as she entered the warehouse.

Ramadan grinned, a small fellow with brown hair and eyes. He looked strong in a neatly ironed shirt. "Welcome, please come in."

We entered a large room with rugs hanging from floor to ceiling, and more rugs rolled and standing upright all around us. Woolen smells of sheepskin permeated the air. The brilliant colors and designs came to life. We sat on French provincial furniture. The wood floor shined.

"What can I show you?" said Ramadan.

"I saw a rug in light beige colors with red accents popping through it." I looked at the rugs surrounding me.

"What size?"

"Five by seven for my entry."

Ramadan brought out many rugs in that size and spread them on the floor. We walked around, eliminating and choosing, until everyone grew hungry.

"We need to get lunch and think about it," Karen said.

"Please, I will buy lunch for you," Ramadan said. "It will be delivered here with wine."

"Great. Let's stay." I melted into the chair.

Ramadan ordered lunch and looked at Bob. "Are you a boxer? You're in great shape."

"I did some boxing in my youth," Bob said.

"I am in training for a tournament at the end of the month. I work hard. Your legs look strong," Ramadan said.

Bob's shorts were his favorite attire, even though he left California years ago. Everyone admired Bob's muscular legs. Men waiting on him in retail stores often asked him if he worked out.

"Every day." And it showed.

Lunch arrived in a feast of platters with meat, cheese, hummus, chicken, peppers, flat bread, rice, vegetables, gyros, and red wine. The smell of cumin and peppers with onion made my mouth water.

"And we haven't even bought anything yet," Bob said.

"Please join us." Andrew motioned to Ramadan.

"No. I am in training, and I must watch my food. Please, enjoy."

"Take a picture of us, Ramadan," Karen said.

Everyone posed at the coffee table for a group picture.

"This is the best meal I've had since we got here," Kristy said.

Everyone drank the red wine except Bob, who preferred white. Wine makes you open your wallet. Ramadan knew this.

After lunch I selected a beige wool rug with thin red flower accents coming to the surface. This satisfied my need for an art piece, hand-made in Istanbul, where I might never visit again.

"I like this rug better than the one at Abraham's, Mom." Kristy walked across the rug. "It's bigger and more colorful."

We settled on the price: twenty-eight hundred dollars.

"Buck will like this one better, too," Bob said.

"Do you need a second rug?" Ramadan said.

"Yes, a smaller one for the landing. Something red, and Kristy needs a rug. She must have a souvenir as well."

Ramadan disappeared and reemerged within minutes holding a small rug on each outstretched arm. "Kristy, if you had to choose, which would you pick?"

Kristy studied each one. "I like the one on the left."

"It's yours, Kristy. It's from the Kurdish region, where I'm from. You will think of me, when you step on it in your house," Ramadan said.

Kristy laughed and accepted the rug.

Ramadan spread other smaller rugs in red for me to choose.

"Do we really need two rugs?" Since Bob didn't drink the wine, he was sober as a judge.

"We need one for the landing. That old red one is no good."

"I like it," Bob said.

He resigned himself to the second rug and offered an opinion. "I prefer that one." He pointed to a blue and red rug with a graphic design.

"I don't know. The colors are a little faded at the top." I said.

Ramadan stood beside me. "That's the dye from plants. It's handmade. There are imperfections."

"What's this rug? The colors are deep red."

"That is a prayer rug," Ramadan said.

"Do we really need a prayer rug?" Bob stood up.

"We might."

"Get the one you like, Judy," Karen said.

I chose the prayer rug. They would ship in two weeks.

"This is Kristy's rug." Ramadan wrapped it, tight and snug with no breathing room. She would take it on board the flight home.

Kristy's phone pinged a message from Bilal. "Are you free for dinner tonight?"

"No. I have plans with my family to see the Whirling Dervish. Sorry, but last night was fun."

Bilal contacted Kristy one more time to say that Ahmed had been murdered last night. It was a street fight, and he was stabbed to death. He forwarded a video from a street camera.

"I saw Ahmed die, Mom. He was such a sweet guy," Kristy said. "We were just three kids out on the town, having fun together, getting to know each other, and now he's gone. It makes me sad."

"I'm sorry you had to see that, Kristy. Now maybe you understand why I was so worried when you were out all night. You can't trust the streets after midnight."

"You were right, Mom," Kristy said through tears. "I probably should not have gone out last night."

Nursing Home Cafeteria

I sit next to my mother at the lunch table in her nursing home, as I do every week (although she claims I only come once a month). She rests her head in her hands and won't look up.

"Mother, would you like me to play the piano? I brought my books."

"Do what you want to do."

"Do you want to stroll around before lunch?"

"Noooo."

"It's a beautiful day outside. Do you want to go for a drive?"

"I can't go outside. I ain't able."

"Mother, I brought you an apple. Do you want some?"

"I don't want no damn apple."

I cut a small piece and peel it. She takes it and eats it, never lifting her head from her hands.

"Do you want me to play?"

"Well, if you're going to, quit assing around and be done with it."

I sit down at the piano next to her. I start with a Patsy Cline song. Some of the residents even applaud. Then I move to a couple of Bob Dylan songs. I only know five songs, so it doesn't take too long for me to finish my whole repertoire.

With lunch over, Mother is ready to go. A couple of wheelchairs are blocking the door. Mother shouts at them to get out of the way. "Go around them if they can't move it," she barks at me.

I wheel her back to the hall.

"Now, push the chair up there and put me to bed. Get on with it."

I lock her chair and stand in front of her, then fold up the footrest and put the stronger of her weak legs on the ground. After circling her arms around my neck, I pull her up and swing her around, pivoting her on her good leg. It isn't very gentle, but it's quick and the best I know how to do.

"You'd never make it in this business," she says as she sits down.

Two years ago at Thanksgiving, everyone was gathered outside my house to say good-bye. I was taking her out of the wheelchair and placing her in the car. With her arms around my neck, I started to pivot her into her seat, when her head hit the doorway. She let go of my neck and dropped down. I hit the ground first, and she landed on my knees. I sat there, holding my mother on my knee and laughing.

"Pick me up and stop laughing," she yelled.

We stayed there with Mother's legs all splayed out, and her diapered bottom resting on my knee. My sister and her husband came to the rescue and lifted her into the car, and I didn't move, laughing like a naughty child. It was the last social event where we could convince Mother to join us. I'd like to think I'm not the reason, but I'm afraid I might be at least partially to blame.

Now, two years later, Mother looks exhausted, but happy to be tucked in, safe and sound. She hasn't been out of the nursing home in two years, but at least she still trusts me to put her to bed.

Descendants

My husband Bob and I passed little flower stands on our way to the William Harris Homestead Heritage Day. On Highway 11, that swath of road between Monroe and Winder, Georgia, where I grew up, my mother's great-grandpa, William Harris, built the homestead on five hundred acres acquired from a treaty with the Creek Indian Nation.

The William Harris Homestead, circa 1825, is one of the few intact plantations remaining in Georgia. He was a farmer, when cotton was king in the South. Over many years in the twentieth century, Hubert Harris grandson of William Harris, obtained the property and continued farming the land.

In 1986, after much research, the farm was placed on the National Register of Historic Places and listed as an Historic Landmark in Walton County. Today, part of the farm is a nonprofit organization. Weddings and school field trips take place there, and every four years the Harris family reunion brings more than two hundred cousins to the grounds for a private picnic and tour. In June 2015, it was open to the public.

Bob and I drove down Highway 11 that morning on our way to the Heritage Day festival. I remembered my first view of that road through the rusted-out floorboard of my dad's 1939 Buick Roadmaster convertible.

***

I could see each stone in the asphalt when the car stopped. The road blurred with dizzying speed when the car took off again. I wanted to know where that road would lead.

"Follow the beer cans to Winder," Uncle Perry Hugh said, because no liquor was sold in Monroe, but Winder had plenty of beer joints. He and my dad frequented those bars or bought moonshine from the local bootleggers. My dad drove to a house deep in the woods for moonshine. Down a dirt road, the house sat in a clearing. It stood on rock pilings. Dogs lounged about in the yard.

"Stay in the car." Dad slammed the door.

My brother Wayne, age eight, my sister Valerie, age four, and I, age six, sat in the back seat of that old car. We peered out the window, as our father walked up the broken wood steps to the porch with no furniture. He disappeared inside the darkness of the open door. After a few minutes, little black faces peeked out. They looked to be our age.

One by one, they stood in the doorway, stuck out their tongue, and disappeared. A barefoot boy came first, maybe eight years old, wearing white shorts and no shirt. Next, came a girl with braids sticking out. She wore a white dress made from a flour sack. We could tell it was once a flour sack because we could see part of the upside down "Pride of Sussex" logo. A younger boy wearing a white shirt and shorts stepped into the doorway, and the little girl came last, a two-year-old, in another flour sack dress. Like the others, she stuck out her tongue, then went back inside.

The kids lined up on the porch, a parade of pink tongues against black faces. We laughed as our father walked down the steps with his purchase.

We called him Dan because Mother did, even though all the church ladies said we would go to hell for calling our father by his first name.

"Never mind those busybodies," Mother had said. "You'll have to do something much worse than that to go to hell." Mother had a way of taking the fear out of life.

Mine was a whiskey-soaked upbringing, probably the reason I enjoy my martini cocktail hour today. Dan also influenced my love for the convertible. My first car was a convertible. He may have been unaware how he influenced my soul searching. While Mother practiced the strict Southern Baptist rules by taking us kids to church, Dan sat on the couch, watching Billy Graham on TV.

I came to believe there was more than one way to find God. I converted to Judaism when I married Bob.

***

"We're here. Slow down," I said.

A police car parked on the side of the road signaled the event with flashing lights. Colorful balloons hung on trees above the barbed wire fence embedded in a mound of kudzu. We drove onto the dirt road full of potholes. Two men in yellow bibs directed us where to park.

I had asked my cousins to meet me at the Heritage Day celebration. We unloaded our picnic and walked across the open field that was once a pasture.

We had driven two hours to see Cousin Ann, who wore a jaunty white hat, sitting in a folding chair under an oak tree near the entrance. I gave her a hug. She had gained weight, and her black hair was now gray on top. She was not the cute little girl that all the boys chased for a kiss. I chased after them, wanting to be kissed, too, but no way, only Ann. No boys wanted to kiss me.

"Your hair is red, and your face is red. You look like an Indian," a boy once told me. In fact, I am $1/16$ Cherokee Indian on my dad's side, and years later that boy would be my first prom date.

Ann had come to the Heritage Day with her two sisters, Brenda and Wanda. They all lived along Highway 11. My sister Valerie and I used to play pretend with Ann and Wanda…

***

"Okay, pretend we live in a castle," I said.

"I'm the youngest and the prettiest," Valerie said. "You're the mean big sister,"

"I have to hide from you," said Ann.

"You be the prince," Wanda said, "and you have to kiss me,"

"You're the mother, and you try to rescue me," said Valerie.

We made up elaborate stories and scripts, and they all hinged on being the youngest and the prettiest.

"Okay, let's play," said Ann.

"I'm the youngest and the prettiest," I said.

***

Whoever shouted that first, of course, had the best part, but the truth was, Valerie was the youngest and the prettiest. Those early days of playing pretend influenced my years in Los Angeles as an actress. I graduated from the University of California, Irvine, with a degree in drama and continued acting for twenty years.

Bob and I were living in California in 1986 when I visited Monroe with my two toddlers. Mother wanted me to see the restoration cousin Dotty's family had begun at the Homestead. Inside the house, a steep, narrow staircase, almost a ladder, took us to the two bedrooms above. I stared out the single window in one small room. The view stretched over the cemetery, and in the distance the cars whizzed by on Highway 11 beyond the trees.

Across the narrow landing, an identical room offered a sweeping view of the dirt road alongside the garden and, a bit beyond, the barn, the corn crib, the smoke house, the blacksmith shop, and the spring house for cold storage of food. The tool shed and salt house were two meager structures farther down the road.

The surrounding fields, once teaming with cotton, now lay fallow. The small dwelling had been constructed for the sustainable lifestyle that existed when William Harris, the original homesteader, my mother's great, grandpa, lived there.

"Do you think Dotty would let me stay here while I'm in town? This would be fun. It has a modern kitchen and bathroom."

"I don't think your kids could manage those steep stairs to the bedroom. They're too little. It would not be safe," Mother had said.

***

Cousin Greg interrupted my thoughts as he embraced me. "Judy, it's good to see you."

Greg and I are the only redheads in the Harris clan of cousins, and we are both writers.

Greg is a stand-up comedian in Atlanta, with a routine about suicide and drug addiction. Not exactly funny, but people can relate to it. We both lost siblings to suicide. Greg's two brothers took their lives, and my sister Valerie did, also.

After my sister's sudden death, I went back to school to learn how to write a book. I was writing my memoir as my capstone for a master's degree in professional writing at Kennesaw State University when Greg asked for my chapter on his family as the introduction to his book, *Heroically Well Adjusted*—a victim's guide to surviving the madness of addiction, the darkness of mental illness, and the horror of suicide for generations to come. The book has since been taken out of publication over family objections.

Greg won a contest for comedians in L.A., and an agent signed him to open for Black comics. He tours the country with Jess Hilarious as the only white face in the show.

He told me he pushed the envelope one evening and insulted someone in the audience, who called him out to fight. He left the show with a bodyguard.

"I want you to come see my routine, but the places I play are pretty rough."

"I've been to urban nightclubs before," I said.

"I'm sure you have. I'll let you know when I play a nicer club. Next weekend, my show has valet parking just down from the Alliance Theater in Atlanta. There's a strip club across the street. You might feel more comfortable coming to that show."

"We'll be out of town next weekend, but I do want to see your act. Keep in touch," I said.

"Ann, let's go up to the farmhouse." I wanted some time with Ann since she was my closest friend from childhood.

"There's no way we're going to his show," Bob said, as he followed us to the house.

We strolled up the grassy hill to the log house with wooden steps and a handrail around the small porch. An antique table held fresh flowers in a washbasin.

"Welcome to the Harris House. Y'all, come on in." A costumed lady in a gingham hoop skirt greeted us with a sweep of her outstretched arm. An old photograph of the original homesteaders, William and Harriet Harris, hangs on the wall right where all visitors cannot miss it.

"Harriet looks just like Valerie, doesn't she?" Ann said.

"Exactly." I studied the face, looking for one more glimpse of my sister who had taken her life four years earlier.

I surveyed the room with its fireplace and remembered Mother pointing to that space in the middle. "My Grandpa was laid out right there in the living room after he died," Mother had said. "I didn't like him. He was mean. We had the same birthday, December 31, and every year we'd load up the wagon and go see him to celebrate our birthdays together. I always dreaded it."

Mother's Grandpa John Lewis Harris, fourth child of William Harris, lived in the homestead until he died in 1929.

Since the modern galley kitchen was closed off for staff only, we strode into the old kitchen with its ladder-back chairs and a rustic table that held plates of dried pears, apples, and figs. At the edge of the room, the steep wooden stairs led us to the bedrooms. A mattress made of cornhusks lay atop a wood-framed bed with an old corset draped over it. Two single beds of similar construction lined the walls of the second bedroom. A handmade quilt was folded on the rattan seat of the single chair. On the desk lay cornhusk dolls, a slingshot, and a hand-carved wooden gun.

We waited for one person at a time to climb back down the stairs, as the Homestead grew crowded with tourists. Outside, on the back porch, jars of jelly from Harriet's garden were stacked for sale on an age-old wood table. In the adjoining field, a mule team plowed.

"Oh my God, my dad used to plow with Ol' Bess," I said.

"I'm going to get an Icee." Ann headed to the venders lined up in the shade.

"Me, too." Bob said.

"Okay, I'll catch up with you. I want to take a picture."

Two large mules harnessed to a plow cut deep and even red furrows through the grass. I hurried over to pet one of them. His heavy feet stamped close to my sandaled foot, and he jerked his head into mine. I smelled his hot horseflesh and remembered that smell and the smell of newly turned earth when Dad plowed. He'd carried me to the garden in a bucket to pick vegetables, one of my first memories. Years later, when he bought a tractor, he had taught me how to plow.

"Gee! Haa! Will you take a picture of me?"

The old man obliged.

I caught up with Bob and Ann back at our little circle of chairs for lunch. As the heat of the day bore down, Ann, Wanda, and Brenda sat fanning themselves with the souvenir, cardboard fans.

"Did you sell Uncle Perry Hugh's house?" I said.

"No. It's not livable," Brenda said.

"How many acres are there with the pond?"

"About fifty," Brenda said. "When Daddy got home from the war, he bought land on both sides of Highway 11 up to Jack Queen's Grocery. He sold the lots to the neighbors, and when he tried to sell one to Mama Harris, she pitched such a fit, he just gave it to her."

My grandmother, Vida Malida Gertrude Perry Harris, was the matriarch of the family, but we called her Mama. At age sixteen, she married twenty-six-year-old Walter Harris, son of John Lewis Harris. They had seven children, two of whom were Ivah Ree (my mother), and Irene, (Greg's mother). As a widow, Mama Harris lived across the road from her oldest boy, Perry Hugh, and his family, including Ann, Brenda, Wanda, Jimmy, and Aunt Dovie.

I remember a cold winter morning, and Mama was sick in bed when I visited her. She tried to teach me how to light the space heater: a large, hissing, gas thing, hot to the touch, when it was on. It was more than I could do. Mama jumped out of bed, her bony feet bouncing across the floor, and lit the heater in a flash.

I can still hear Mama's footfalls on the frozen linoleum floor. She had a little hitch in her step. She jumped back into bed just as fast saying, "If you want something done, you have to do it yourself."

Words to live by.

"You're better than the whole lot of them," she once told me.

Maybe she felt sorry for me because I didn't make the grades my siblings made, or I didn't get the attention my pretty sister got, but she made sure I knew I was her favorite—probably the reason I had the confidence to work as a flight attendant for United Airlines, move to California, and leave that Southern lifestyle behind.

Mama had strength and ability, and she dressed for work in the fields. No skin was exposed to the sun. She wore a floppy hat, a long-sleeved shirt, long pants, and gloves. She even tied a scarf around her neck. Her children worked the fields, too. She weighed only ninety pounds, but with rapid-fire hands, she picked two hundred pounds of cotton a day. We cousins picked cotton together, but not like her. We only did it to earn money for the fair. Six cents a pound was the going rate. The rides at the fair were twenty-five cents each, so all we needed was four dollars. That was a little over sixty-five pounds, and it might take us a week to collect.

After a hot day in the cotton fields, we'd go swimming in Uncle Perry Hugh's pond. I learned to swim in that water, so muddy I couldn't see the bottom. I waded out, tiptoeing through the fine silt. The warm liquid layer floated on top of the cold mushy bottom. An occasional fish nudged my legs and gave me a start.

"Come on, Judy, just keep kicking your legs and moving your arms—keep your head up," my brother Wayne shouted.

I propelled myself a short distance treading water, till I learned to put my head down, feet up, and stroke. That lesson took. I am a year-round lap swimmer today.

Swimming in the Harris' pond, which is just a few miles over the hill from the Homestead, is one of my most idyllic memories of a long hot summer with no cares in the world. These images play in my mind like an old movie. Maybe that's because I am the lone survivor of my parents and siblings.

I was living in California when my brother was the first death in the family at age twenty-seven. He died from an infection in 1975. He didn't make it to the Bicentennial in 1976. That's how I remembered the date. My first life shock, the death that nothing can fix. I have never felt more helpless, but many years later when my sister took her life, I experienced that helplessness again.

When my brother died, I felt resentful that I was not told for three days because I was working as a flight attendant on a trip to Pittsburgh. Mother called Bob and, between the two of them, they decided to wait till I was back home in California to deliver the news.

When I got to Mother's house, she was crying out of control, and I sat there like a stoic and wouldn't go to her. Bob looked at me and motioned with his head for me to go to her, but I wouldn't. I was mad at him, too, for not calling me on my trip. I was so angry and self-absorbed, as my sister would say. Those were her favorite words to describe me.

It was a terrible day. He should not have died. I had just seen him on a trip to Atlanta two weeks before, and he was fine.

He had flu symptoms and went to the doctor for treatment, but he got worse. Three days later my mother took him to the emergency room, and he died the next day. We never received an autopsy report, and he was cremated. The death certificate said it was an infection, but no one knew what it was. Maybe it was a matter of finding the right doctor. But I took it hard. Compared to my sparkling new life in California, their world seemed far away, and so was their reality.

***

Cotton Gin, Circa 1905, Georgia

"BLAM!"

A gunshot interrupted my thoughts.

"We need to see the reenactment," I said.

"I'm staying here." Wanda said. "I know how it ends."

Bob and I followed Ann and Brenda to the edge of the woods where a large crowd had gathered to hear the Confederate soldier describe the Kennesaw Mountain Battle. The skirmish began as Rebels ran over the hill to barricades and shoveled dirt to fortify the logs. The Yanks loaded their muskets with powder using a large plunger. Then, "BLAM!"

"Damn, that's loud," I said.

"That soldier must be a Harris. Look at his face," Brenda said. "He favors Daddy,"

"He does look like a young Perry Hugh," I said.

"I think most of the volunteers in costume here today are Harrises," Ann said.

After a few minutes of deafening shots, I wanted to get back to our chairs before people headed for the exits.

Across the muddy expanse, Dotty's voice came over the microphone at the bandstand, thanking everyone for coming out. We caught up with her by the Creek Indian dancers, who were dressed in colorful loincloths.

"Judy, I'm so glad y'all came." Wearing a Calico dress and a straw hat, Dotty smiled, her blue eyes sparkling. "We're photographing the descendants at 3:00 at the house." She glanced at her watch. "That's in twenty minutes," she said, as she turned to go.

"We have time to go to the cemetery," I said.

A wrought iron fence surrounds the burial grounds. The family has traced its history to the Revolutionary War. Thomas Harris was a patriot in the War of Independence in 1776 and is buried in Virginia.

In 2007, The Daughters of the American Revolution were in attendance at the Harris family reunion for a ceremony to return soil from the grave of the oldest known Harris descendant's grave in Virginia to the Harris Homestead cemetery, situated on the edge of Highway 11. From the distance came the sounds of cars passing by as each cousin scooped a small shovel of dirt from the bucket of soil and placed it onto the site marked in history at the William Harris Homestead—Thomas Harris 1738-1821. It reminded me of a Jewish burial where each member of the deceased's family scoops a shovelful of soil onto the casket.

I have mixed feelings when I visit the Homestead. I remember what my sister Valerie said when I asked why she didn't go to the Harris family reunions anymore. "I know who we are."

Now I know, too.

Of course, plantation owners in the South pre-Civil War also owned slaves.

In writing this story, I interviewed cousin Dotty who confirmed that fact. At first I felt shock, disbelief, and shame. Certainly the Harris log cabin was not Tara in *Gone with the Wind*, but it stood as an historic preservation of a sustainable life style in its darkest days of enslaved people. In 1825, these people lived by candlelight and horse and buggy, so, yes, those were dark days.

When I first moved back to the South and saw the reenactments of the Civil War, I thought they were a joke. "They're still fighting that war," I said with a laugh, because it seemed foreign to me after living in California for twenty years.

Today, as a descendant of people who owned slaves, I feel embedded in the history of the South and of this country. Maybe even my view of the Civil War has changed. It seems more personal now. My people were under

attack, Northern Aggression they called it, where before, it was just history.

As I walk the grounds of the plantation, I wonder where the slaves were housed. The structures are not there anymore, but today are part of an archeological survey. Eighteen people were enslaved in 1850 and ten in 1860. Those are the census records, according to Cousin Dotty.

Georgia seceded from the Union in 1861 and was the last former Confederate state to be readmitted to the Union in 1870.

I try to understand the system of the plantation. In 1821, the South was agricultural, and cotton was the main product. John Harris, father of William Harris, lived in Oglethorpe County, Georgia, and he owned a cotton gin. He was a businessman who used the means available to him to grow his business, and that was slavery. According to records, he had fifteen children, and he bequeathed slaves to his first five children.

The Harrises were prodigious. William Harris, the youngest of John Harris, had eleven children, and John Lewis Harris, the fourth born of William Harris and my mother's grandpa, had sixteen children. Lots of field hands for their agrarian lifestyle.

William Harris did not inherit his slaves. Did he think he was rescuing these poor Black people he purchased in the 1840s? Was he giving them room and board for their labor? I'm not sure he believed that at all. According to an Estate Sale in 1842, The Hire of One Negro Boy by William Harris for $13.18 was paid to his brother Jourdan's estate.

The slaves had been in the South for 200 years already, having arrived on the first slave ship to Virginia to build the colony in 1619. The African Americans came with the Europeans to settle this nation, though the Africans were enslaved.

Sad to say, it was the lifestyle of the South for 246 years.

Even my father, Dan Coker, claims kin to the plantation. His uncle, Early Coker, married Florine Harris, daughter of John Lewis Harris, my mother's grandpa. Both Uncle Early and Aunt Florine are buried at the Homestead.

I wonder if the Black man my dad bought liquor from that day when I sat in the back seat of that old car, was descended from one of the Harris slaves. Maybe my dad knew that, and liquor brought them together.

I imagine most slaves, once they were freed, stayed near the plantation;

the only home they had known for twenty years, while some may have ventured up North. No records or diary entries of the slaves of the Harris House have been found and no graves, however, through collaboration with the Georgia Gwinnett College Anthropology program and the Gwinnett Archaeological Research Society, the William Harris Homestead is using archaeology to learn about the lives of the enslaved individuals who lived there so that their memories are honored and their stories are incorporated into the narrative of the property.

Learning about the slaves at my Great-Great Grandpa's farm has given me a new outlook on the African-American man's story. The three kids who integrated Monroe High School in 1964 could have descended from the Harris Plantation.

In 1947, Minnie, the Black maid, walked up and down Highway 11, helping new moms with their babies and housework. Perhaps Minnie was descended from the Harris slaves.

"She put Wayne back in diapers, and he was doing so good on the pot," Mother whined.

We had no money to give her, just food and clothing. There were many Harrises and Cokers living on Highway 11, so she found work.

I feel bad for the Creek Indians who were moved to make room for the white settlers after the war of 1812. The United States government was trying to build a country and develop the land at the cost of indigenous people and slaves. Now I'm part of that story.

We take pride in tracing our family to the Revolutionary War in 1776 that started a new nation. The War of 1812 with England, France, Canada, and the Indians resulted in the William Harris Homestead from a treaty with the Creek Indian Nation. Including the slave trade and the Civil War, the Harris families were here for it all. Today, we come together in a shared history to commemorate the life of the Harris family, flawed as it may be. Lessons can be learned at the Harris House.

I had gotten as far away as I could from the South: moved to California, even changed my religion. Then Dotty shouted, "Descendants! Descendants!" for all the family to gather for a picture.

"Descendants! Descendants!" she called.

And that's me.

Zoom Passover

This year was different from all other years. The COVID-19 Pandemic had engulfed the country for five weeks, and now we were sheltering in place. Face masks and gloves were *de rigueur*. Businesses closed, and people were unemployed. Hospitals were overrun with sick and dying patients and running out of supplies. Panic food shopping and hoarding of toilet paper were the norm as grocery stores were lined with empty shelves. Afraid to spread the disease by close contact with people, supermarkets offered delivery until those services were exhausted.

I had to go to the market myself, and I waited until the cupboards were bare to venture out.

"Are you going to put your laptop on the dinner table?" my husband Bob said.

"Yes, and I'm going to scan and send the Haggadah to the kids."

"It sounds like too much trouble."

"Kristy wants to do it. She'll send us the link. Brett's up for it, but he is three hours earlier in L.A. Shayne says she hasn't done Passover in years. She lives alone with her little dog. I think she would enjoy the whole family gathering. I picked up matzah at Publix along with matzah ball soup mix. I still have one apple left, and I have honey and nuts, so I can make haroset."

What else goes on the Seder plate?

I took out the thirty-page Haggadah that Grandpa Hal, Bob's father, gave me years ago when we lived in California. We had not hosted Passover with other families since Kristy was in college. On occasion, Bob and I were invited to a friend's Seder, or we went to the temple Seder. I laughed, remembering Brett as a little boy grabbing a cup for a drink and choking on the wine. Since there were no wine glasses at the temple service, he thought apple juice was in that plastic cup.

***

"Tonight would be different from all other nights," is a quote from the Haggadah. A child or an inquisitive person would ask four questions: "Why is this night different from all other nights?" and with each question, the story of the Exodus of the Jewish people from Egypt was told.

This year the days of affliction are upon us once again, and there is a new plague: the novel corona virus. The washing of hands has never been more important, and it is part of the Seder ritual from thousands of years ago.

I didn't have all the symbolic food for the Seder plate that Kristy made when she was nine years old. For the lamb bone, I substituted a piece of coral. I had matzah, but I had no other bread in the house, so we ate matzah all week in the Passover tradition. For the bitter herb, horseradish was squeezed from a bottle onto the plate. A boiled egg and salt water, I had. For parsley, I substituted rosemary.

At 7:30 p.m. on the east coast, our children Zoomed into the quartered frame of my laptop. Bob and I in one, Kristy and her boyfriend Carlos, who observed Passover for the first time, in the next frame, Shayne and Rascal the Pomeranian who rested on the sofa beside her, then Brett and his roommate Bocz, who poked his head in the last frame to say hello and disappeared.

A ski slope from Aspen was Kristy's background. We had cancelled a family trip to Aspen because of COVID, and Kristy cried. The groomed corduroy hill beckoned. Then she switched the scene to a Jacuzzi filled with young people, and she disappeared into the picture as if dunking into the water only to reappear for our entertainment—virtual reality at its best.

I lit candles that stood in the candleholder, which we bought in Safed when we visited Brett for Passover during his study abroad in Israel. Bob and I led the Seder, and the kids participated with their Haggadah on a split screen. We drank wine—Brett had a margarita, and I opened the door for Elijah. We said Kadesh, and the service usually concludes with "Next year in Israel," but we ended with a joke and a hope, "Next year in Aspen."

Although we were miles apart—Miami, Los Angeles, New York, and Cartersville—we felt close. Four screens attached on a computer, talking, laughing, praying, and observing a time gone by in history, yet feeling its relevance today. It was the Happy Pandemic Passover I will always remember.

Marilyn

Since the COVID-19 Pandemic lockdown started in the last few weeks of March 2020, I had not talked to Marilyn, my dear friend in California who had cancer.

"Hey girl, are you under house arrest?" I said with a giggle.

"Judy, I'm in hospice at home for a week now. Both my sisters are here, and Katie is here with my two grandkids. They take turns sleeping with me. I have a bed set up in the great room. John still sleeps upstairs."

Marilyn talked without taking a breath, as I tried to absorb all that she said. "You're in hospice? I thought you were in treatment at UCI Medical."

"Yes. I love my doctor. He's been great, but he said the chemo was making it worse, and I should go home. He told me there's no cure, and he talked to Katie and John, and now everyone is on the same page. I'm in fifth stage hospice, so I can call a staff of people 24/7 who come to take care of me, or be with me." Marilyn's voice was animated, almost excited. "They asked if I wanted a chaplain. I couldn't think who I wanted to talk to—maybe an Indian Gandhi type. What would he say?"

"I remember you went on several spiritual retreats over the years."

"Judy, you know I've always been interested in different religions. Then I said, 'send me a rabbi.' "

"You asked for a rabbi?"

"And, Judy, she came today, a lady rabbi from L.A., and she was great. She told me her whole story, and I asked her to sing two songs that I knew from the Jewish religion."

"The Mi Shebeirach," I said. "The prayer for healing."

"Yes," Marilyn said. "She told me there is a sect of Jewish people who believe in the afterlife, and another group who don't."

I thought she was talking about the Messianic Jews, who believe in the afterlife, also known as Jews for Jesus, of which I am not one.

"Do you have a church, Marilyn? Didn't Katie go to Trinity Methodist Preschool, when my kids went to Temple Bat Yahm?" I said.

"Yes. But we never went to church. I just didn't believe it. I grew up Methodist, but I never went back," she told me. "Judy, I'm afraid of the darkness."

"What do you mean?"

"You know… at the end," she said. "The rabbi told me that I have experienced the darkness before and to think back, when it went black. And, Judy, remember when I was on that weird diet, when I didn't eat all day for weeks?"

"Yes." I laughed. "You only drank chicken broth, and when you went out to dinner with Karen and me, you drank a beer, but you didn't eat. You were worried that people would think you were eccentric because you didn't eat. Remember what I said?"

"Yes. You said, 'They don't care.' "

We laughed, and it felt good to laugh at the morbidity.

"But, Judy, it would go black sometimes."

"It did? Because you didn't have enough fuel?"

"Yes. So I remember the black, and I'm not afraid of it anymore because I know it."

"Wow." I didn't know what else to say.

She wanted to talk about dying and transitioning, but I didn't know how. I just listened to her voice, enjoying her words over the phone. I wanted to be there to comfort her, but I lived across the country in Georgia.

"Judy, you remember my friend Jennifer. You got into a fight with her about Trump," Marilyn said.

"Oh, yeah. Gale and I ganged up on her. Tell her that I said Trump is doing a helluva job."

I knew that Jennifer was there every day and had been driving Marilyn to chemo. That should have been my job. "Marilyn, I'm coming to see you. I want to help you."

"No. Judy, don't come now. The house is full. Both my sisters are here. There're too many people. It's not a good time."

My connection to Marilyn withered in my hand as the light on my phone turned off. I was losing her, and my eyes burned. She had called for a rabbi for her last rites. *Did I influence that call?*

When we lived in Newport Beach, California, her family had come to Shayne's Bat Mitzvah, when our girls were best friends in seventh grade. Maybe that service had moved and influenced her to seek a rabbi in her dying days.

I had to sound the alarm to all my friends in Newport Beach who knew Marilyn. I called Gale, another friend in our group, and explained that Marilyn was in hospice.

"If you want to come to California, you can stay with me," she said.

I was torn. Should I risk getting on an airplane and being stranded there during the COVID-19 lockdown? There were worse places to be stranded.

My son the actor said, "Just go, Mom. If it will help you. Just go. Get on an airplane. You can come to L.A. and see me."

"And sleep on the couch with you?" I laughed.

Brett had just moved to L.A. and was sleeping on his friend's couch.

"Yeah," he said.

Should I take the advice of a thirty-one-year-old who thought the way I had when I was that age?

I called Karen, the psychologist in our group.

"Just sing to her and pray for her," she said in her lilting voice.

"No. That's not enough."

"Would you feel better if you made a reservation on Delta for a future date?" she said.

"Yeah, give Delta some more money to hold for you," my daughter Shayne said, when I told her Karen's suggestion. Shayne was referring to the trips we cancelled on Delta and got only a credit and not a refund.

I continued to ask everyone, "What should I do?"

Bob said, "I can't tell you what to do, Judy. You know that."

He was right. Only I could make the decision in my best interest and in Marilyn's best interest. Was I being selfish? Yes. I was.

My frustration grew as I remembered our first conversation about her illness. It was in January, when she had pain, and she went to different doctors trying to get a diagnosis. It took a few weeks.

"Marilyn, I'm planning a girl's trip," I had said. "Meaning, I'm coming to L.A. to see all my girlfriends. I want to stay at Pelican Hill."

"Oh yeah, Pelican Hill is a beautiful golf resort overlooking the ocean."

"I didn't know they had golf there, but it overlooks Crystal Cove where we hiked six miles one day. I found a one-bedroom suite for five hundred dollars a night for New Year's, but I couldn't talk Bob into it. He didn't want to go back, since we were just there in August, when we saw you and John. So I'm coming by myself this time, and we'll get together."

"Don't forget the cabins at Crystal Cove. It's a state park now, but you have to book a year in advance."

"There's always the Little Inn by the Sea," I said.

We laughed, remembering the Little Inn on Newport Boulevard, a block off the beach. I stayed there when my girlfriends could not put me up or just to have my own place. It was small and old, offering a honey bun and coffee for breakfast, and beach equipment. You only had to cross the Boulevard. I had chosen a second-floor room with a view of the ocean through the many sailboat masts that blotted the sky. It was affordable for that coastline.

"Yeah, you better stay there first before you go to Pelican Hill," Marilyn said. "But, Judy, let me get through this before you come. I don't want to be sick. Wait a few months."

"Okay, but I want to see you," I said.

Did I really want to see her that way?

I have known Marilyn for almost forty years. As newlyweds, Bob and I lived in The Park Newport Apartments on the Back Bay. I played tennis with Donna Dodd who introduced us, and Marilyn and I have been friends since our daughters were in diapers.

In the '80s, I was a flight attendant and Marilyn and Donna sold real estate. The three of us took long lunches at The Ritz in Fashion Island. A waitress bumped my head with her tray and gave me a champagne shampoo. We laughed as I dried my hair with a napkin and continued the lunch. We ate salads and drank Dom Pérignon for hours.

Those were the kind of girl gatherings we enjoyed. No wonder I went back there every chance I got. My kids grew up on the beach. The beaches of Southern California were my favorite because they felt like home. The Pacific had big waves, and the water was cold, reaching only seventy degrees in the summer, but my kids jumped in and boogie-boarded. Kristy, my middle child, won a boogie board contest at Emerald Bay.

When we got there, along with Marilyn's family, the contest had already begun. Kristy grabbed her board and ran out to the waves, riding one after another, not realizing she had crashed a contest. When she came dripping out of the water, carrying her board, the judges, sitting at the table, jumped up to give her a trophy. "You won second place. Congratulations."

Kristy accepted the trophy with a surprised smile.

Marilyn and I were housewives, and taking the kids to the beach was a lifestyle. We arrived around 3:00 p.m., when most people were leaving, and the hottest part of the day was past. The kids swam in the crashing waves and built sand castles, using palm fronds that dotted the shore at Emerald Bay.

The bathroom had a million-dollar view—up the many rustic steps to the toilets housed in two buildings that looked like shacks. That view from the railed balcony was unparalleled. As far as the eye could see—deep blue Pacific Ocean melded into sky blue dotted with seagulls. And on a clear day, Catalina Island, only twenty-six miles away, loomed on the horizon.

As the sun sank in the western sky, we packed up our beach supplies and trudged up the steep wooden stairway to the top of the cliff overlooking the ocean. The handrails were full of splinters. My oldest, Shayne, caught a splinter deep in her hand, causing it to bleed. From then on, the beach was known as "Blood Beach."

The kids were small—Brett was three, Kristy was seven, and Shayne was ten. After we climbed the stairs from Blood Beach, the playground was hard to resist. The kids sat atop the jungle gym or flew high on the swings. Marilyn and I watched, maybe with a glass of wine, until the sun set. What a way to spend the day.

We showered off by the bathhouse and piled into the Volvo station wagon for a ride to McDonalds for dinner with Marilyn and Katie in tow. Those were the days.

I remembered Bob and me smoking joints with John and Marilyn and cracking up at the name of the Ben and Jerry's Chunky Monkey Ice Cream that we ate. Bob was surprised they smoked pot, too. "They didn't seem the type," he said.

John was a landscape architect and a sculptor in works of alabaster. Some of his art was displayed in the local shops. Marilyn played her baby grand like a concert pianist, and she studied hypnosis to help people stop smoking.

Years later, when Marilyn and I talked on the phone, she said she was moving a friend into the Oasis Senior Center.

"Why is she moving there?"

"Because she's a senior citizen, Judy, and so are we."

"Oh, yeah. We are. When did that happen?"

"Not too long ago," she said.

More recently, when we talked prior to her illness, she mentioned that the bus picked up the seniors and took them to the dispensary to get their marijuana.

"Wow. California is so different now," I said. "We had to get it from Uncle David.

After twenty years in that setting, Bob and I moved to Georgia for his business, and the kids grew up. But I never lost my love of California. When Bob traveled, I got on an airplane and flew back and stayed with Marilyn or Karen or Gale—whoever was willing to put me up.

Marilyn has been gone from this earth now for ten months, and I still have not made it back to California.

The Pandemic fog hung over us like the clouds over Newport Harbor as the sail boats bobbed and weaved against the pier.

"Will you take a picture of us?" I handed my phone to the waitress at the Rusty Pelican. We posed for a picture on that pier, not knowing it would be our last.

Acknowledgments

Thanks to my editors, Shayne Benowitz and Donna Jones. Thanks also to Kennesaw State University and Adina Jocelyn Langer, curator of the Museum of History and Holocaust Education at Kennesaw State University where my mother's story and her WWII US Navy WAVES raincoat and hat are on display. Thank you to the writers groups from the Osher Lifelong Learning Institute (OLLI) Kennesaw State University, and thanks to the Cartersville writers group, Atlanta writers critique group, and to Treaty Oak Publishers.

My experiences as related in this book are true. Some of characters are literary creations and fictional in certain aspects.

It is my wish to honor the colorful characters in my stories and the friends and family who walked this earth with me by putting them on the page so their lives endure.

After getting as far away as I could from Highway 11, I have returned to Georgia. As I sit on the banks of the Etowah River, the organic smell is the same as Uncle Perry Hugh's pond. It is springtime, and the bumblebees buzz, signaling it's time to go barefoot. Highway 11 is nearby, as it cuts across the state of Georgia. It cuts through my memory of where it all started and will always be a little piece of me.

A Note About The Author

Judy Benowitz is a creative writer in Cartersville, Georgia, with an MA in Professional Writing from Kennesaw State University in Georgia, where she was Who's Who among Students in American Universities and Colleges in 2016. She is the 2015 Creative Writing Contest winner in The Georgia Writers Museum, and her stories appear in GRITS (*Girls Raised in the South*), the *Atlanta Jewish Times*, and the Georgia Writers Association among others.

Made in United States
Orlando, FL
29 October 2023